TWELFTH EDI

ACCOUNTANTS'
HANDBOOK

2013 SUPPLEMENT

TWELFTH EDITION

ACCOUNTANTS' HANDBOOK

2013 SUPPLEMENT

LYNFORD GRAHAM

WILEY

Published by John Wiley & Sons, Inc., Hoboken, New Jersey.

Published simultaneously in Canada.

Limit of Liability/Disclaimer of Warranty: While the publisher and author have used their best efforts in preparing this book, they make no representations or warranties with respect to the accuracy or completeness of the contents of this book and specifically disclaim any implied warranties of merchantability or fitness for a particular purpose. No warranty may be created or extended by sales representatives or written sales materials. The advice and strategies contained herein may not be suitable for your situation. You should consult with a professional where appropriate. Neither the publisher nor author shall be liable for any loss of profit or any other commercial damages, including but not limited to special, incidental, consequential, or other damages.

For general information on our other products and services or for technical support, please contact our Customer Care Department within the United States at (800) 762-2974, outside the United States at (317) 572-3993 or fax (317) 572-4002.

Wiley publishes in a variety of print and electronic formats and by print-on-demand. Some material included with standard print versions of this book may not be included in e-books or in print-on-demand. If this book refers to media such as a CD or DVD that is not included in the version you purchased, you may download this material at http://booksupport.wiley.com. For more information about Wiley products, visit www.wiley.com.

Library of Congress Cataloging-in-Publication Data:

ISBN 9781118752326 (Paperback)

Printed in the United States of America
10 9 8 7 6 5 4 3 2 1

CONTENTS

PREFACE

The twelfth edition of *Accountants' Handbook* continues the tradition established in the first edition nearly 90 years ago of providing a comprehensive single reference source for understanding current financial statement and reporting issues. It is directed to accountants, auditors, executives, bankers, lawyers, and other preparers and users of accounting information. Its presentation and format facilitate the quick comprehension of complex accounting-related subjects updated for today's rapidly changing business environment.

This work is the first supplement to the twelfth edition. It adds several new chapters on contemporary accounting issues from new authors to the existing 43 chapters, and provides a partial update to several chapters to reflect important changes since the compilation of the twelfth edition.

The most important force in shaping future accounting practice is the degree to which international accounting perspectives will be incorporated into the U.S. accounting framework. Reluctance to subjugate accounting standards setting and regulatory mandates in the United States to international determination continues to deter integration of current U.S. generally accepted accounting principles (GAAP) and international practice.

References to the professional accounting literature in this edition continue to include references to the new Financial Accounting Standards Board Codification (Accounting Standards Codification, or ASC) in each chapter, where applicable. Sometimes the original literature is also cited, where it can be helpful in understanding the development of thought and can help orient us to the prior literature.

In this supplement we have included a new chapter explaining XBRL reporting by Clinton (Skip) White, a recognized expert in this area. The desire for more comparability in financial reporting has led to a worldwide movement to create taxonomies to classify reporting captions for easier machine readability and cross-company comparisons. Will the permission for companies to create unique tags when the taxonomies do not reflect the exact nature of a specific reported value lessen the potential value of this tool? Time will provide more answers as taxonomies evolve and companies evolve their accounting systems. One thing seems clear: SEC mandates for public companies to report in this format will ensure that evolution and refinement will continue.

Two new chapters are contributed by Les Livingstone, a recognized expert in a number of disciplines. His chapter on the Balanced Scorecard helps readers understand this widely utilized management tool for assessment and enhanced performance planning. Using accounting information internally for management purposes is a valuable perspective, as external reporting alone is not a sufficient description of the value of accounting data. Adding to that perspective is a new chapter on product costing and assigning indirect costs to manufactured products. This continues to be a challenging area for many businesses, and Les provides insight into the complexities of the financial reporting and management uses of this information with clarity in exposition. We welcome these new perspectives in this supplement and for future editions.

In addition, we have provided here new chapters updating certain perspectives and portions of specific chapters in the twelfth edition. Rather than republishing an entire chapter, this format allows for a more concise exposition of important recent changes. Partial updates are provided for five chapters:

- Chapter 7: Introduction to Internal Control Assessment and Reporting
- Chapter 12: Revenues and Receivables

- Chapter 31: Real Estate and Construction
- Chapter 33: State and Local Government Accounting
- Chapter 38: Estates and Trusts

The specialized expertise of the individual authors remains a critical element in this edition, as it has been in all prior editions. Although the editor worked with the contributing authors, in the final analysis each chapter is the work of and presents the viewpoint of the individual author or authors.

ABOUT THE EDITOR

Lynford Graham, CPA, PhD, CFE, is a Certified Public Accountant with more than 30 years of public accounting experience in audit practice and national policy development groups. He is a visiting professor of accountancy and executive in residence at Bentley University in Waltham, Massachusetts. He was a partner and the director of audit policy for BDO Seidman LLP, and was a national accounting and Securities and Exchange Commission consulting partner for Coopers & Lybrand, responsible for the technical issues research function and database, auditing research, audit automation, and audit sampling techniques. Prior to joining BDO Seidman LLP, Dr. Graham was an associate professor of accounting and information systems and a graduate faculty fellow at Rutgers University in Newark, New Jersey, where he taught financial accounting courses. Dr. Graham is a member of the American Institute of Certified Public Accountants and a past member of the AICPA Auditing Standards Board. He is a Certified Fraud Examiner and a member of the Association of Certified Fraud Examiners. Throughout his career he has maintained an active profile in the academic as well as the business community. In 2002 he received the Distinguished Service Award of the Auditing Section of the American Accounting Association. His numerous academic and business publications span a variety of topical areas, including information systems, internal controls, expert systems, audit risk, audit planning, fraud, sampling, analytical procedures, audit judgment, and international accounting and auditing. Dr. Graham holds an MBA in industrial management and a PhD in business and applied economics from the University of Pennsylvania (Wharton School).

ABOUT THE CONTRIBUTORS

Michael A. Antonetti, CPA, CMA, is a partner with Crowe Horwath LLP. He has over 20 years of experience providing assurance and business advisory services to clients in many industries, including manufacturing, distribution, banking, professional services, transportation, and hospitality. Mr. Antonetti's experience includes assisting clients with merger, acquisition, and divestiture transactions and application of related accounting standards. He also serves clients with international operations in Europe, Asia, and North and South America.

Yogesh Bahl, CPA, MBA, has more than 18 years of experience in leading global forensic investigations, delivering dispute consulting services, and helping companies manage enterprise risks. He leads the National Life Sciences practice and the Northeast Antifraud practice. He specializes in assisting companies manage issues involving accounting, third parties, strategic alliances, and intellectual property. He has helped companies address and resolve multimillion-dollar issues involving accounting and finance, business partner reporting, unclear contract terms, and supply chain infiltration. In addition, his experience includes strengthening the financial and audit-related provisions in various types of agreements, including licensing, collaboration, distribution, and co-promotion agreements. By leveraging his advisory experience with corporations, he is effective when testifying on industry practice, breach of contract, accounting, and intellectual property matters.

Noah P. Barsky, PhD, CPA, CMA, is an associate professor at the Villanova School of Business. He earned his BS and MS in accounting from The Pennsylvania State University and his PhD from the University of Connecticut. His professional experience includes practice in the fields of accounting and finance as an analyst, auditor, and business consultant, as well as instructional design and delivery for global professional services firms. He has been recognized with multiple national and international awards and grants for his scholarly writing and curriculum innovation.

Neil Beaton, CPA, ABV, CFAI, ASA, MBA, is a managing director with Alvarez & Marsal Valuation Services in Seattle, Washington. He specializes in the valuation of public and privately held businesses and intangible assets for purposes of litigation support (marriage dissolutions, lost profits claims, and others), as well as acquisitions, sales, buy-sell agreements, employee stock option plans (ESOPs), incentive stock options, and estate planning and taxation. He also performs economic analysis for personal injury claims and for wrongful termination and wrongful death actions. His primary areas of concentration are valuations of early-stage, venture-backed company and litigation support across a broad spectrum of financial and economic matters. With more than 23 years of valuation and litigation support experience, Mr. Beaton has been involved in valuing companies in all major industries and has provided expert testimony in a number of domestic and international venues. Prior to joining Alvarez & Marsal, Mr. Beaton spent nine years with Grant Thornton, where he most recently served as the Global Lead of Complex Valuation. He is a co-chair of the AICPA's Valuation of Private Equity Securities Task Force and a member of the AICPA's Mergers & Acquisitions Disputes Task Force. He is a member of the Business Valuation Update Editorial Advisory Board and is on the Board of Experts, *Financial Valuation and Litigation Expert*.

Benedetto Bongiorno, CPA, CRE, has more than 40 years of public accounting experience providing auditing, accounting, and consulting services to both public and private real estate companies. He has served as national director of real estate for Deloitte & Touche and BDO, and has many years of experience in research and practical application of specially developed substantive analytical audit procedures and technologically based tools. He has made major contributions in public accounting, both in real estate and financial audits and in the field of continuous audit. As a cofounder and head of audit and accounting consulting services at Natural Decision Systems, Inc., he was awarded U.S. patents in both continuous assurance and internal control. Mr. Bongiorno continues to apply his extensive expertise in improving real evaluation techniques, transparency, and cost-effective auditing strategies through consulting for public accounting firms as well as both public and privately held companies.

Brad A. Davidson, CPA, is partner in charge of the Securities and Exchange Commission (SEC) competency center of the national office of Crowe Horwath LLP. The Assurance Professional Practice group (or national office) has responsibility for technical consultations, quality control, and communications of current SEC and accounting developments. Brad specializes in the financial institutions industry. He serves as Crowe's representative to the Center for Audit Quality's SEC Regulations Committee, which meets quarterly with SEC staff to discuss emerging financial reporting issues. In December 2010, Brad served as steering committee chair of the American Institute of Certified Public Accountants' annual national conference on current Securities and Exchange Commission and Public Company Accounting Oversight Board developments. Earlier in his career, he completed a two-year professional fellowship with the AICPA in Washington, D.C.

Jason Flynn, FSA, MAAA, is a principal in the Human Capital Total Rewards practice at Deloitte Consulting LLP, where he provides broad technical guidance and advisory consulting with regard to pension and retiree medical benefit plans to a wide spectrum of clients, including multinational clients. He serves as a national leader for Deloitte Consulting's retirement practice.

Sydney Garmong, CPA, is partner in the audit practice with Crowe Horwath LLP located in Washington, D.C. Her primary responsibility is to address accounting and regulatory issues affecting financial institutions. She is a member of the American Institute of Certified Public Accountants Depository Institutions Expert Panel, which maintains an ongoing liaison with various regulatory and standard-setting agencies that impact financial institutions, including the federal bank regulators, the Securities and Exchange Commission, and the Financial Accounting Standards Board. In addition to addressing technical issues, Sydney is a frequent speaker at industry and regulatory conferences. Prior to joining Crowe Horwath, she was a senior manager at the AICPA in Washington, D.C. During her time with the AICPA, she addressed financial institution and financial instrument accounting, auditing, and regulatory matters.

Martha Garner, CPA, is a managing director in PricewaterhouseCoopers' national office specializing in health care, not-for-profit, and governmental accounting and financial reporting matters. She currently chairs the American Institute of Certified Public Accountants' Health Care Expert Panel and has served on numerous Financial Accounting Standards Board, Government Accounting Standards Board, and AICPA task forces and committees. She is a contributing author for *Montgomery's Auditing* (John Wiley & Sons, 1998) and the *Financial and Accounting Guide for Not-for-Profit Organizations* (John Wiley & Sons, 2012), and is the author of articles and publications on a variety of accounting topics.

Timothy Geddes, FSA, MAAA, is a senior manager in the Human Capital Total Rewards practice at Deloitte Consulting LLP, where he provides broad technical guidance and advisory consulting with regard to pension and retiree medical benefit plans to a wide spectrum of domestic and multinational clients. He serves on the American Academy of Actuaries Pension Committee and has spoken at numerous national actuarial meetings.

Frederick Gill, CPA, is senior technical manager on the Accounting Standards Team at the American Institute of Certified Public Accountants, where he provides broad technical support to the Accounting Standards Executive Committee. During his more than 20 years with the AICPA, he participated in the development of numerous AICPA Statements of Position, Audit and Accounting Guides, Practice Bulletins, issues papers, journal articles, and practice aids. He was a member of the U.S. delegation to the International Accounting Standards Committee, represented the U.S.

accounting profession on the United Nations Intergovernmental Working Group of Experts on International Standards of Accounting and Reporting, and was a member of the National Accounting Curriculum Task Force. Previously he held several accounting faculty positions.

Alan S. Glazer, PhD, CPA (inactive), is the Henry P. and Mary B. Stager Professor of Business at Franklin & Marshall College, Lancaster, Pennsylvania. He was associate director of the Independence Standards Board's conceptual framework project and has been a consultant to several AICPA committees. His articles on auditor independence, not-for-profit organizations, and other issues have been published in the *Journal of Accountancy*, *CPA Journal*, *Issues in Accounting Education*, *Accounting Horizons*, and other academic and professional journals. He is also coauthor of a three-volume series of portfolios on financial statement analysis published by Bloomberg BNA.

Lynne M. Glennon, CPA, MST, is a full-time instructor for DePaul University's Master of Science in Taxation program. She currently teaches accounting for income taxes, transactions in property, and taxation of corporations and shareholders on campus as well as online for a national CPA firm. Prior to teaching full-time, she worked in both industry and public accounting for 20 years as a tax director and tax consultant. As director of tax planning for Global Hyatt Corporation, she was primarily responsible for tax planning support on large-scale restructurings and mergers, acquisitions and dispositions, and management and control of the federal audit process, including communications with the Internal Revenue Service. As senior manager in Deloitte & Touche's lead tax services group, she focused on corporate and partnership taxation and served a number of multinational clients in the manufacturing, distribution, and service industries. Ms. Glennon is a Certified Public Accountant in the State of Illinois and a member of the American Institute of Certified Public Accountants. She is a graduate of the University of Notre Dame with a BA in economics; her MST degree is from DePaul University.

Bill Godshall, CPA, joined Frazier & Deeter's assurance practice in 2005 and serves as the lead partner for the assurance group's quality control function. Since joining Coopers & Lybrand in 1990, Bill has had extensive experience in the energy and mining sector of assurance practices at two international accounting firms. He has worked on oil and gas audit and attestation engagements, utility audits, controls projects, attestation engagements, and mining joint venture costs reviews. He also assisted his energy and mining clients with special accounting and auditing projects in the areas of derivatives, asset retirement obligations, leasing, and other complex topics. Mr. Godshall spent two years at the Public Company Accounting Oversight Board, where he authored the inspection guidance for derivative accounting and auditing areas that is still in place today. In addition, he led the inspection of the audits of several energy and natural resource Securities and Exchange Commission issuers.

Richard A. Green, CPA, has over 25 years of auditing, accounting, and consulting experience, including all phases of external and internal auditing. Mr. Green leads the Sacramento public sector assurance practice of Macias Gini O'Connell LLP. He served on the Governmental Accounting Standards Board Task Force on Pension Accounting Research and was recently appointed to the American Institute of Certified Public Accountants' State and Local Government Expert Panel Pension Comment Letter Task Force. Mr. Green is the engagement partner on the largest pension plan in the nation, the State of California Public Employees' Retirement System.

Frank J. Grippo, MBA, CPA, CFE, is an associate professor of accounting at William Paterson University in Wayne, New Jersey. He earned his BS in accounting from Seton Hall University and his MBA from Fairleigh Dickinson University. Prior to teaching, he was an auditor with Arthur Andersen & Co. His firm performs financial and accounting consulting for various nonprofit organizations, specializing in internal control structures, auditing, and fraud detection. Clients include well-known health and welfare, religious, and educational organizations.

Wendy Hambleton, CPA, is an audit partner working in the National SEC Department in BDO Seidman LLP's Chicago office. Prior to joining the SEC Department, Ms. Hambleton worked in the firm's Washington, D.C., practice office. She works extensively with clients and engagement teams to prepare SEC filings and resolve related accounting and reporting issues. Ms. Hambleton coauthors a number of internal and external publications, including the AICPA's *Guide to SEC Reporting* and Warren Gorham & Lamont's *Controller's Handbook* chapter on public offering requirements.

Philip M. Herr, JD, CPA, PFS, is a senior case design analyst in the advance markets unit of AXA Equitable Life Insurance Company located in New York City. He is a former adjunct professor at Fairleigh Dickinson University, School of Continuing Education, and New Jersey City University. Mr. Herr specializes in the areas of tax; estate and trusts; business succession and planning; personal financial planning; Employee Retirement Income Security Act issues and transactions; retirement, employee benefit, and executive compensation planning; and the use of life insurance, annuities, and insurance products. He is admitted to the New York and U.S. Tax Court Bars and is a member of the New York State Bar Association, American Institute of Certified Public Accountants, New York State Society of Certified Public Accountants, and Association for Advanced Life Underwriting. He holds life, health, and variable insurance licenses in New Jersey and New York and Financial Industry Regulatory Authority 7, 24, 55, 63 and 65 securities licenses.

Frank Hydoski, PhD, is a director in the New York Forensics & Dispute Services practice of Deloitte Financial Advisory Services LLP. He is responsible for developing new products and approaches in forensic accounting and investigations for clients in both the private sector and the public sector. Mr. Hydoski is internationally recognized for his work in complex investigations, especially those requiring information technologies to facilitate forensic analysis. He was the chief investigator examining the United Nations Oil-for-Food Programme and led a crucial part of the massive forensic effort in the investigation of Holocaust-era accounts held by Swiss banks.

Henry R. Jaenicke, PhD, CPA, was the C. D. Clarkson Professor of Accounting at Drexel University. He is the author of *Survey of Present Practices in Recognizing Revenues, Expenses, Gains, and Losses* (FASB, 1981) and is the coauthor of the twelfth edition of *Montgomery's Auditing* (John Wiley & Sons, 1998). He has served as a consultant to several American Institute of Certified Public Accountants committees, the Independence Standards Board, and the Public Oversight Board.

Richard R. Jones, CPA, is a senior partner in the National Accounting Standards Professional Practice Group of Ernst & Young LLP, where he is responsible for assisting the firm's clients in understanding and implementing today's complex accounting requirements. Mr. Jones's fields of expertise are in the areas of impairments, equity accounting, real estate, leasing, and various financing arrangements.

Tom Jones was the vice chairman of the International Accounting Standards Board from its founding in 2001 until 2009. Prior to this he was a trustee and vice chairman of the Financial Accounting Foundation, which oversees the Financial Accounting Standards Board. He was a member of the Investor Task Force and was chairman of the American Bankers Association CFO Committee. He has been elected to the Financial Executives International Accounting Hall of Fame. Mr. Jones's corporate experience includes 20 years with Citibank/Citicorp as executive vice president and principal financial officer. He previously served for 15 years with IT&T in Italy, Belgium, and New York.

Ira G. Kawaller is the founder and principal of Kawaller & Co., a boutique consulting firm that specializes in assisting commercial enterprises with their use of derivative contracts. He is also the managing partner of the Kawaller Fund. He can be reached at Kawaller@kawaller.com; additional biographical information about Dr. Kawaller can be accessed at http://kawaller.com/wp-content/uploads/2012/08/Ira_Kawaller_Vita.pdf.

Darin W. Kempke, CPA, is a partner at KPMG LLP in its Philadelphia office. He is the national audit sector leader for KPMG's power and utility practice. He has been working with power and utility clients (regulated and nonregulated) all over the world in his 21-plus years in the industry both with Arthur Andersen LLP and currently with KPMG LLP. He specializes in business and accounting services to regulated and nonregulated energy companies, provides energy thought leadership for publications and the KPMG Global Energy Institute, and is a frequent speaker on the power and utility conference and webinar circuit. He spent time in the KPMG LLP Department of Professional

Practice working on energy issues, including derivatives, leases, emissions, and variable interest entities. He is a Certified Public Accountant licensed in Missouri, Kansas, New York, New Jersey, Pennsylvania, and the District of Columbia. He is a graduate of the University of Kansas with a BS in accounting and a BS in business administration.

Cynthia L. Krom, PhD, CPA, CFE, is assistant professor of accounting and organizations at Franklin & Marshall College, Lancaster, Pennsylvania. She is active in the New York State Society of Certified Public Accountants as well as the American Accounting Association. She has published articles in professional journals on the Bank Secrecy Act and terrorism financing, and her research interests include strategic bankruptcy and accounting history.

Richard F. Larkin, CPA, is technical director of not-for-profit accounting and auditing for BDO USA, LLP, in Bethesda, Maryland. Previously he was the technical director of the Not-for-Profit Industry Services Group in the national office of PricewaterhouseCoopers. He is a Certified Public Accountant with over 40 years of experience serving not-for-profit organizations as independent accountant, board member, treasurer, and consultant. He teaches, speaks, and writes extensively on not-for-profit industry matters and is active in many professional and industry organizations. He has been a member of the Financial Accounting Standards Board Not-for-Profit Advisory Task Force and the American Institute of Certified Public Accountants Not-for-Profit Organizations Committee, and chaired the AICPA Not-for-Profit Audit Guide Task Force. He participated in writing both the third and fourth editions of *Standards of Accounting and Financial Reporting for Voluntary Health and Welfare Organizations*, and the AICPA Practice Aid *Financial Statement Presentation and Disclosure Practices for Not-for-Profit Organizations* (1999). He graduated from Harvard College and has an MBA from Harvard Business School. He is a coauthor of the fourth, fifth, and sixth editions of *Financial and Accounting Guide for Not-for-Profit Organizations* (John Wiley & Sons).

Elizabeth Lindsay-Ochoa, JD, LLM (Taxation), is a Vice President, Senior Trust Counsel for Tompkins Financial Advisors. Her primary focus is trust and estate planning. Her specialties include trust administration to help clients meet wealth and estate planning goals; wealth protection and transfer; philanthropy, including charitable giving strategies that align with investment objectives; estate settlement and administration, preserving estate value and minimizing family and heir burden; and family governance. She has written articles for the *Tax News Quarterly*, *Probate and Property*, and *National Underwriter*. Liz received a bachelor of arts degree in telecommunications from Michigan State University and her Juris Doctor from Thomas M. Cooley Law School, Lansing, Michigan. Additionally, she earned her LL.M. in Taxation at the University of Denver, Colorado. She is a member of the Colorado and Michigan Bar Associations and the National Committee on Planned Giving. She also holds her Financial Industry Regulatory Authority (FINRA) Series 7, 66, and 24 securities registrations.

Les Livingstone, MBA, PhD, CPA, is the MBA Program Director in Economics, Finance, and Accounting at the University of Maryland, University College, a leading university with 100,000 students, including 3,000 MBA students. He earned MBA and PhD degrees at Stanford University and is a CPA (licensed in New York and Texas). Since 1991 he has directed his own consulting firm, specializing in damage estimation for large-scale commercial litigation and in business valuation. He is the author of many books and professional articles. His website is at http://leslivingstone.com.

James Mraz, CPA, MBA, is a professor of accounting and business at the University of Maryland, University College. He has taught accounting and business for over 30 years in several colleges. He has also conducted accounting accuracy reviews for John Wiley & Sons since 2005 and completed the instructor's manual for Prentice Hall's Accounting Information System's textbook. Mr. Mraz was a government auditor for 33 years while serving in the Marine Corps, Department of Health and Human Services, and the Department of Defense. He also served as chief financial officer for a resale and recreation government organization.

Grant W. Newton, PhD, CPA, CIRA, is a professor of accounting at Pepperdine University. He is the author of the two-volume set *Bankruptcy and Insolvency Accounting: Practice and Procedures:*

Forms and Exhibits, Sixth Edition (John Wiley & Sons, 2006) and coauthor of *Bankruptcy and Insolvency Taxation, Second Edition* (John Wiley & Sons, 1994). He is a frequent contributor to professional journals and has lectured widely to professional organizations on bankruptcy-related topics.

Don M. Pallais, CPA, has his own practice in Richmond, Virginia. He is a former member of the American Institute of Certified Public Accountants Auditing Standards Board and the AICPA Accounting and Review Services Committee. He has written a host of books, articles, and continuing professional education courses on accounting topics.

Cynthia Pon, CPA, has over 20 years of professional experience providing auditing, accounting, and consulting services to the private and public sectors. Ms. Pon leads the San Francisco Bay Area Public Sector Assurance practice of Macias Gini O'Connell LLP, bringing extensive experience in federal, state, and local financial and compliance auditing. She is experienced in the application of generally accepted accounting principles and has been recognized by the Governmental Accounting Standards Board for her leadership in assisting California governments with early implementation of its standards. Ms. Pon also serves on the Government Finance Officers Association Special Review Committee for Comprehensive Annual Financial Report awards and has instructed numerous governmental clients on a variety of accounting and audit issues and challenges.

Zabihollah Rezaee, PhD, CPA, MBA, is the Thompson-Hill Chair of Excellence and Professor of Accountancy at the University of Memphis and has served a two-year term on the Standing Advisory Group of the Public Company Accounting Oversight Board. He received his BS degree from the Iranian Institute of Advanced Accounting, his MBA from Tarleton State University in Texas, and his PhD from the University of Mississippi. Professor Rezaee holds a number of certifications, including Certified Public Accountant, Certified Fraud Examiner, Certified Management Accountant, Certified Internal Auditor, Certified Government Financial Manager, Certified Sarbanes-Oxley Professional, Certified Corporate Governance Professional, and Certified Governance Risk Compliance Professional. He has also been a finalist for the SOX Institute's SOX MVP 2007, 2009, and 2010 Award. Professor Rezaee has published over 180 articles in a variety of accounting and business journals and made more than 200 presentations at national and international conferences. He has also published seven books: *Financial Institutions, Valuations, Mergers, and Acquisitions: The Fair Value Approach* (John Wiley & Sons, 2007); *Financial Statement Fraud: Prevention and Detection* (John Wiley & Sons, 2002); *U.S. Master Auditing Guide, Third Edition* (Commerce Clearing House, 2004); *Audit Committee Oversight Effectiveness Post-Sarbanes-Oxley Act* (Bloomberg BNA); *Corporate Governance Post-Sarbanes-Oxley: Regulations, Requirements, and Integrated Processes* (John Wiley & Sons, 2007); *Corporate Governance and Business Ethics* (John Wiley & Sons, 2008); and *Financial Services Firms: Governance, Regulations, Valuations, Mergers and Acquisitions* (John Wiley & Sons, 2011).

Francis E. Scheuerell, Jr., CPA, is a managing director at Navigant Consulting and is a Certified Public Accountant and certified management accountant. He has almost 30 years of diverse business experience in all areas of financial management and technical accounting, including accounting for business combinations, restatements, corporate restructurings, spin-offs, inventory, leases, revenue recognition, income taxes, equity method investments, segments, and consolidations, including variable interest entities. He has extensive experience addressing accounting and reporting issues for the real estate, construction, health care, hospitality, software, entertainment, retail, and manufacturing industries. Mr. Scheuerell has served as an interim executive and/or consultant for numerous billion-dollar companies facing complex and extensive financial reporting issues. He has managed teams restating financial results and rebuilding financial reporting infrastructures while helping to restore regulator and investor confidence in those organizations. He has represented and testified on behalf of clients at Securities and Exchange Commission and NASDAQ hearings. Additionally, he has served as an expert witness in a securities litigation case. He has assisted numerous clients with their initial public offering or private place memorandums. Mr. Scheuerell is an accomplished public speaker and author of numerous articles, publications, and continuing professional education seminars. He was a Project Manager—Research and Technical Activities for the Financial Accounting Standards Board and is a graduate of Illinois State University.

Jae K. Shim, PhD, MBA, is a professor of accounting and finance at California State University, Long Beach, and chief executive officer of Delta Consulting Company, a financial consulting and training firm. Dr. Shim received his MBA and PhD degrees from the University of California at Berkeley (Haas School of Business). He has been a consultant to commercial and nonprofit organizations for over 30 years. Dr. Shim has also published numerous articles in professional and academic journals and has over 50 college and professional books to his credit.

Reed K. Storey, PhD, CPA, had more than 30 years of experience on the framework of financial accounting concepts, standards, and principles, working with both the Accounting Principles Board, as director of Accounting Research of the American Institute of Certified Public Accountants, and the Financial Accounting Standards Board, as senior technical advisor. He was also a member of the accounting faculties of the University of California, Berkeley; the University of Washington, Seattle; and Bernard M. Baruch College, City University of New York, as well as a consultant in the executive offices of Coopers & Lybrand (now PricewaterhouseCoopers LLP) and Haskins & Sells (now Deloitte & Touche LLP).

B. Scott Teeter, MBA, CMA, is the vice president of land acquisition and development for the Austin/San Antonio, TX, division of Ryland Homes. He earned his BS in finance from The Pennsylvania State University and his MBA from the Wharton School of the University of Pennsylvania.

Daniel Thomas, EA, MAAA, is a specialist leader in the Human Capital Total Rewards practice at Deloitte Consulting LLP, where he serves as an actuarial specialist for the Deloitte audit teams and as a technical resource and reviewer within Deloitte's pension actuarial practice.

George I. Victor, CPA, is a partner in Giambalvo, Stalzer & Company, CPAs, P.C., and is the firm's director of quality control, where he is responsible for formulating the firm's accounting and auditing policy standards, including monitoring, consulting, technical research, staff training, and review of completed engagements. Mr. Victor has extensive experience in providing accounting and advisory services to both privately held and Securities and Exchange Commission–reporting companies. He also provides consulting services in areas of quality control, U.S. generally accepted accounting principles, and International Financial Reporting Standards matters to other certified public accounting firms in the United States and abroad. He is a member of the American Institute of Certified Public Accountants as well as the New York State Society of CPAs, where he serves as a member of its board of directors, has chaired various committees, and serves as a member of the Editorial Board of the *CPA Journal*. He is an adjunct professor at the City University of New York. Mr. Victor has been published or quoted in various professional journals and books and frequently lectures on accounting- and auditing-related topics.

Caroline H. Walsh, CPA, has over 33 years of specialized experience in auditing and consulting for local government agencies, nonprofits, and corporate enterprises. Ms. Walsh serves as the Quality Control Partner at Macias Gini O'Connell LLP and leads the firm's Professional Standards Group. From October 2006 through 2009, Ms. Walsh served on the American Institute of Certified Public Accountants American Institute of Certified Public Accountants State and Local Government Expert Panel, where her role was to provide review and technical support services for the public accounting profession, including drafting and updating the AICPA guides for Audits of State and Local Governments and Government Auditing Standards and Circular A-133 Audits. Since 2009, Ms. Walsh has participated on the Expert Panel Task Force, which reviews and comments on the recent Governmental Accounting Standards Board (GASB) due process documents related to accounting and reporting for pension benefits. In 2009, she was appointed for a three-year term to the GASB Advisory Committee, a standing committee whose members review the GASB staff's annual proposed changes and additions to the GASB's *Comprehensive Implementation Guide*.

Clinton E. White, Jr. (Skip), MBA, DBA, is the Associate Chair for MIS in the Department of Accounting and MIS at the University of Delaware and the author of *The Accountant's Guide to XBRL* and *The Guide & Workbook for Understanding XBRL* (www.skipwhite.com). Professor White has published numerous articles in academic and professional journals, conducted numerous academic and professional workshops around the world, and was the founding Webmaster for the American Accounting Association. His recent efforts have been focused on XBRL and other emerging XML-based technologies and their effect in various areas of business. He has held faculty positions at Pennsylvania State University (1981–1987) and the University of Delaware (1987 to present). He received his BA in history and government from Western Kentucky University (1969), MBA from the University of Louisville (1975), and DBA from Indiana University (1981). He served as a Military Intelligence Specialist in the First Special Action Force—Southeast Asia (1969–1971) and worked as a branch manager and loan officer at a savings and loan in Louisville, Kentucky (1974–1977). For details, visit www.lerner.udel.edu/faculty-staff/faculty/clinton-white.

Jan R. Williams, PhD, CPA, is the Ernst & Young Professor and Dean, College of Business Administration, at the University of Tennessee. He is past president of the American Accounting Association and a frequent contributor to academic and professional literature on financial reporting and accounting education. Most recently he has been involved in the redesign of the CPA Examination and is a frequent speaker on this and other topics of professional significance.

David M. Zavada, CPA, MPA, is a partner with Kearney & Company in Alexandria, Virginia, where he specializes in providing accounting and audit services to the federal government. He is a former chief of the Financial Standards and Grants Branch within the Office of Federal Financial Management at the Office of Management and Budget, and deputy to the Controller of the U.S. Government. He was director of the Office of Financial Management at the Department of Transportation, Federal Aviation Administration, and served as the Assistant Inspector General, Office of Audits at the Department of Homeland Security. In all of these positions he played a leadership role in developing and implementing government-wide financial management policies.

Mark L. Zyla, CPA/ABV, CFA, ASA, is managing director of Acuitas, Inc., an Atlanta, Georgia–based valuation and litigation consultancy firm. As a valuation specialist, he has provided consulting for numerous valuations in financial reporting and other types of engagements. He was the 2011 chair of the American Institute of Certified Public Accountants National Business Valuation Conference and presented AICPA's Fair Value Measurement Workshop. He is the author of *Fair Value Measurement: Practical Guidance and Implementation, Second Edition* (John Wiley & Sons, 2012).

XBRL REPORTING IN THE EDGAR DATABASE (NEW)

Clinton E. White, Jr., MBA, DBA

University of Delaware

4a.1 INTRODUCTION

The eXtensible Business Reporting Language (XBRL) is an open specification and a global standard for representing business financial information in computer-readable form. I like to describe it as an XML (eXtensible Markup Language) vocabulary for exchanging financial information. XML is a set of rules and syntax, a meta-language, describing a standard format for computerized documents and their processing. Since its debut as a standard in 1998, it has rapidly become the language for exchanging data between software packages on computer networks, including the Internet. XBRL was first introduced in 2001 and rapidly evolved in parallel with the sophistication of XML processing languages into its current version (2.1) in 2005. Because it enables standardized computerized reports that can be validated, regulatory bodies around the world took interest and began projects to investigate its capabilities and implement projects. Early adopters include the Dutch Taxonomy Project (2004) to streamline business regulatory reporting; the U.S. Federal Deposit Insurance Corporation (FDIC) (2005) for bank call reports; the Australian Standard Business Reporting Program (2006) to reduce the burden and cost to business of multiagency regulatory reporting; and the U.S. Securities and Exchange Commission (SEC) pilot interactive data project (2005), a voluntary SEC filings project. Today, all publicly traded companies reporting under U.S. generally accepted accounting principles (GAAP) are including their financial statements in XBRL format with their SEC 10-Q and 10-K documents, and regulatory bodies, stock exchanges, and governments around the world are implementing XBRL filing projects.

While each regulatory agency or government body implements XBRL in its own way, there are a number of significant advantages to having companies report their operational and financial information in XBRL format. First, in the case of the SEC, each piece of information is tagged with a standard tag selected from the U.S. GAAP XBRL taxonomy or from an appropriate extension taxonomy (discussed in section 4a.3). For example, a company reporting "gross profit" in an income statement would tag its reported value with the standard U.S. GAAP XBRL tag name **GrossProfit**. There are over 16,000 tag names in the U.S. GAAP 2012 XBRL taxonomy, each representing a financial reporting concept. When tagged, each reported "fact" becomes searchable, reusable, comparable to others, and unambiguously interpretable by a human or a computer program; tagging will be illustrated in more detail later. Second, the choice of tag names is the province of the company doing the reporting and should therefore better reflect what is actually being reported. Data aggregators have been using their own proprietary tagging for years, but when doing so they have to normalize each individual company's reported data so that it will fit into predefined categories; unique, company-specific data is forced into general buckets (e.g., revenue) and lost for all practical purposes. Third, companies must tag every "fact" reported in the footnote disclosures as well as the line items on the face of the financial statements. As a result, an unprecedented amount of extremely granular data will be available to the user and analyst. Other advantages will be noted in this chapter, along with issues that have arisen as a result of the SEC and the Financial Accounting Standards Board (FASB) closely monitoring and suggesting improvements in financial reporting in XBRL format.

This chapter is devoted to an introduction to standardized financial reporting in XBRL format, the U.S. GAAP XBRL taxonomies, and the issues surrounding the use and usefulness of the XBRL-formatted financial information. In this chapter, you will be introduced to XBRL financial statements through the documents and interactive tools available in the SEC's EDGAR database. The objectives are to help you understand XBRL documents, the available interactive data tools, and the complexities of SEC filings. This chapter is designed to be read while seated at an Internet-connected computer. At the end, you will be introduced to several new, recently released taxonomies for corporate actions, governance, risk and compliance, and inline XBRL.

4a.2 A FIRST LOOK AT THE SEC EDGAR DATABASE

For each 10-Q and 10-K in the SEC EDGAR database, there is now a set of "document format files" and a set of "data files." This chapter is an interactive tour of the SEC's EDGAR database and its contents. To start, point your browser to http://sec.gov/edgar/searchedgar/companysearch.html, and choose a company (e.g., type IBM in the *CIK* or *Ticker Symbol* box) and *click* Find Companies. The result should be similar to Exhibit 4a.1. We use IBM as an example of a sophisticated company with experience reporting in XBRL format starting in 2009.

Next, to find the actual documents, click the Documents (Documents) button next to an

Interactive Data (Interactive Data) button. The result should be similar to Exhibit 4a.2.

The Document Format Files are the standard HTML and text files containing the filed SEC document (i.e., 10-Q or 10-K) and its accompanying exhibits in humanly readable format. As you can tell from the Description column, the first Document is the actual 10-K filing. Many companies include their financial statements in their 10-Q or 10-K document, but others, including IBM, include them by reference; IBM's financial statements and notes are found in EX-13. Data files are the XBRL instance document and its supporting schema and other documents in computer-readable format, explained in detail in this chapter. What this means for a user of the EDGAR database is that a publicly traded company's financial statements are now available as a computer-readable XBRL document, as well as a Web page (HTML). The XBRL instance document is meant to be "consumed" by a software application so that its contents can be accessed directly for analysis purposes, and its data reused in another application or loaded into a preferred analysis application (e.g., an Excel spreadsheet). As discussed in more detail later, analysts find an individual company's XBRL instance documents useful for digging in depth and analyzing a company across time periods, as opposed to comparisons across multiple companies.

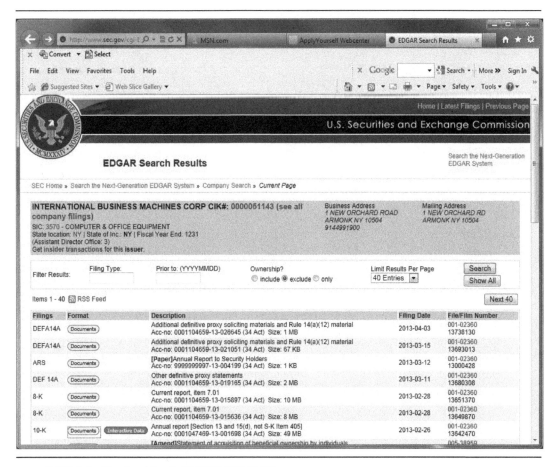

Exhibit 4a.1   Edgar Search Results (IBM 10-K 2013-02-26)

4a.3 XBRL TAXONOMIES AND VIEWING TOOLS

XBRL is an XML (eXtensible Markup Language) vocabulary that defines "elements" (aka tags), their relationships to each other, how they are calculated and presented on financial statements, and the document structure for financial reporting in XBRL format. The 2012 U.S. GAAP XBRL taxonomy defines over 16,000 accounting and financial reporting concepts as XML elements. Taxonomies are made up of XML schemas and linkbases. Without getting bogged down in technical details, each element is defined in the U.S. GAAP XBRL taxonomy schema by assigning a unique name, data type, and accounting-specific attributes to a financial reporting concept such as gross profit. In the U.S. GAAP XBRL taxonomy schema, **GrossProfit** is an element name with a "monetary" data type (i.e., it is measured in a currency), reported on an income statement for a duration of time, with a normal credit balance. Gross profit is further defined in XBRL presentation, calculation, and reference linkbases as a part of "operating income" on an income statement calculated as the result of subtracting "cost of revenue" from "revenues." XBRL taxonomies function as dictionaries for looking up element names for financial reporting concepts to be used in XBRL-formatted financial statements.

Filing Detail

Search the Next-Generation EDGAR System

SEC Home » Search the Next-Generation EDGAR System » Company Search » Current Page

Form 10-K - Annual report [Section 13 and 15(d), not S-K Item 405] SEC Accession No. 0001047469-13-001698

Filing Date 2013-02-26 | Period of Report 2012-12-31
Accepted 2013-02-26 15:35:35 | Filing Date Changed 2013-02-26
Documents 21

Interactive Data

Document Format Files

Seq	Description	Document	Type	Size
1	10-K	a2212340z10-k.htm	10-K	307966
2	EX-10.1	a2212340zex-10_1.htm	EX-10.1	37852
3	EX-10.2	a2212340zex-10_2.htm	EX-10.2	14168
4	EX-12	a2212340zex-12.htm	EX-12	25478
5	EX-13	a2212340zex-13.htm	EX-13	6548699
6	EX-21	a2212340zex-21.htm	EX-21	63512
7	EX-23.1	a2212340zex-23_1.htm	EX-23.1	3617
8	EX-24.1	a2212340zex-24_1.htm	EX-24.1	65098
9	EX-24.2	a2212340zex-24_2.htm	EX-24.2	2537
10	EX-31.1	a2212340zex-31_1.htm	EX-31.1	7869
11	EX-31.2	a2212340zex-31_2.htm	EX-31.2	7859
12	EX-32.1	a2212340zex-32_1.htm	EX-32.1	4753
13	EX-32.2	a2212340zex-32_2.htm	EX-32.2	4823
20	G283352KI21I001.GIF	g283352ki21i001.gif	GRAPHIC	11225
21	G283352KI23I001.JPG	g283352ki23i001.jpg	GRAPHIC	1467
	Complete submission text file	0001047469-13-001698.txt		49290046

Data Files

Seq	Description	Document	Type	Size
14	EX-101.INS	ibm-20121231.xml	EX-101.INS	10472589
15	EX-101.SCH	ibm-20121231.xsd	EX-101.SCH	179447
16	EX-101.CAL	ibm-20121231_cal.xml	EX-101.CAL	187730
17	EX-101.DEF	ibm-20121231_def.xml	EX-101.DEF	931413
18	EX-101.LAB	ibm-20121231_lab.xml	EX-101.LAB	3055843

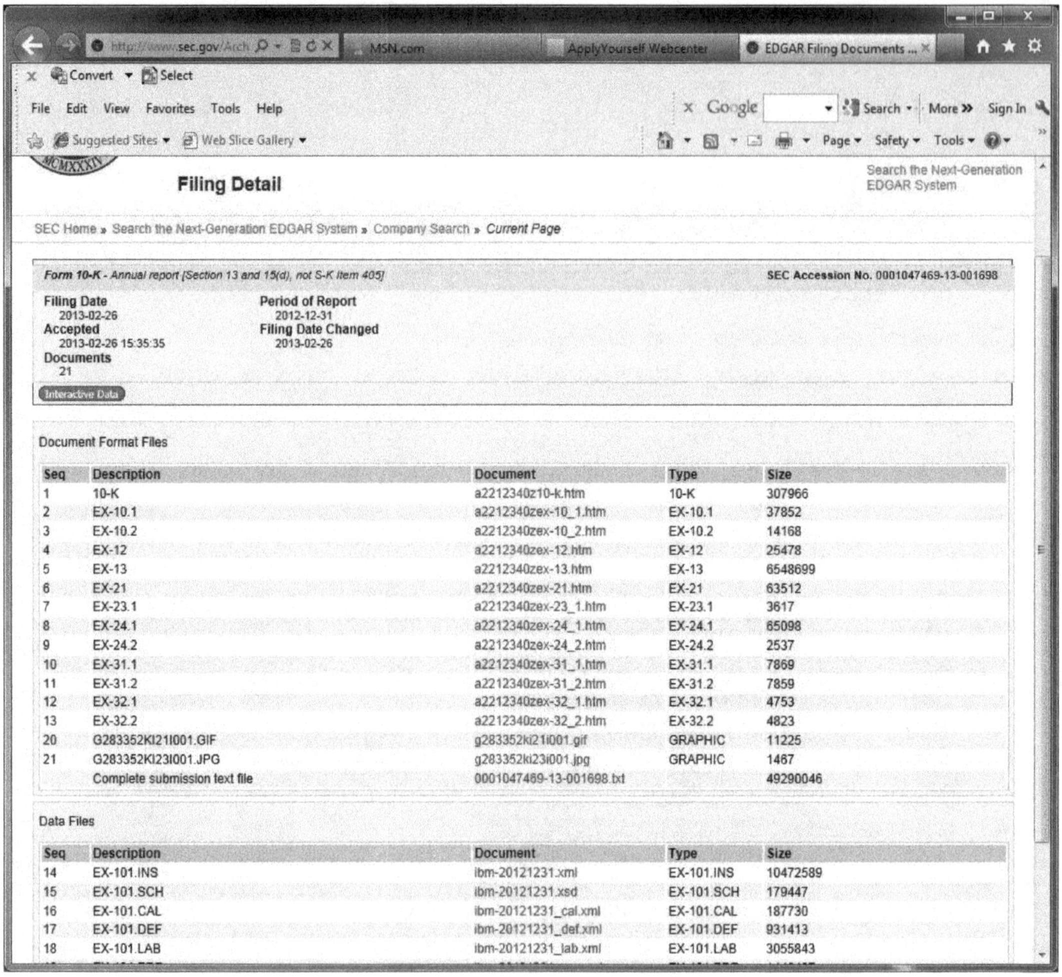

Exhibit 4a.2 IBM's 10-K EDGAR Filing Detail (2012-12-31)

An XBRL-formatted financial statement is referred to as an "instance document" because it is an instance of the class of XML documents defined in the XBRL specification (i.e., the specification that defines the XBRL vocabulary). Every XBRL instance document must be connected to an XBRL taxonomy that supports it (i.e., an XBRL taxonomy in which all of the elements that are found in the instance document are defined). Instance documents are the subject of the next section.

U.S. GAAP XBRL reporting to the SEC involves the standard U.S. GAAP XBRL taxonomy and extension taxonomies. Every SEC filer is expected to create an XBRL "extension" taxonomy to support its instance document. An XBRL extension taxonomy extends the standard U.S. GAAP taxonomy for an individual company's financial reporting situation. For example, each company must choose an industry entry point into the U.S. GAAP taxonomy (i.e., Commercial and Industrial, Banking and Savings Institutions, Brokers and Dealers, Insurance, or Real Estate). By choosing an entry point, a company selects a subset of the U.S. GAAP taxonomy that contains element names, financial statements, and disclosures commonly used by companies in that category. Further, within each category, a company designates the type of financial statements it is using (e.g., a classified or unclassified balance sheet and an income statement including or excluding gross margin).

Each company submits its extension taxonomy along with its instance document for storage in the EDGAR database.

To illustrate these points, return to the SEC's EDGAR company search page by pointing your browser to http://sec.gov/edgar/searchedgar/companysearch.html, choose a company (e.g., IBM), and scroll down to the first item with an Interactive Data **Interactive Data** button and *click* it. You should see an interactive data index page similar to Exhibit 4a.3. This page is actually a browser interface on top of a company's XBRL instance document. Notice that it contains SEC-specific "Document and Entity Information" that must accompany a filing, as well as the financial statements, notes, tables, and additional details about the financial statements.

Next, *click* on Financial Statements and choose the Consolidated Statement of Earnings, and you should see an income statement similar to Exhibit 4a.4.

Next, *click* the first line item (services revenue) and you should see the definition of this item from the XBRL taxonomy supporting this statement (i.e., IBM's extension XBRL taxonomy). If you then *click* the + sign beside the **Details** link, you should see the specific XBRL definition from the XBRL taxonomy schema (similar to Exhibit 4a.5).

The definition for an element describes in accounting-relevant terms the concept that the element represents. Every element in the U.S. GAAP XBRL taxonomy has a definition, and it is the first piece of evidence that a document preparer should use to determine which element name to use to tag a reported value. In addition, a user of this interactive data viewer can check the item to

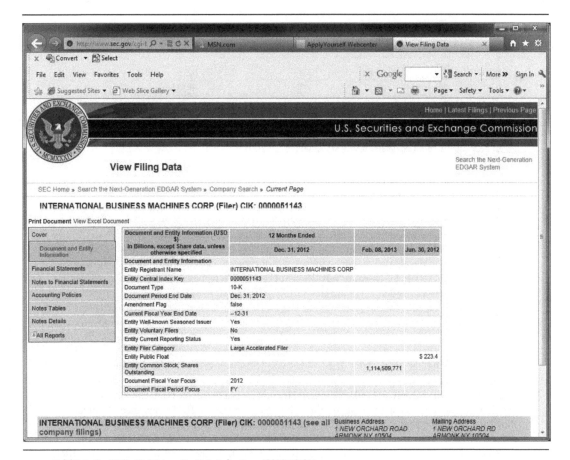

Exhibit 4a.3   IBM's 10-K Interactive Data Index Page (2012-12-31)

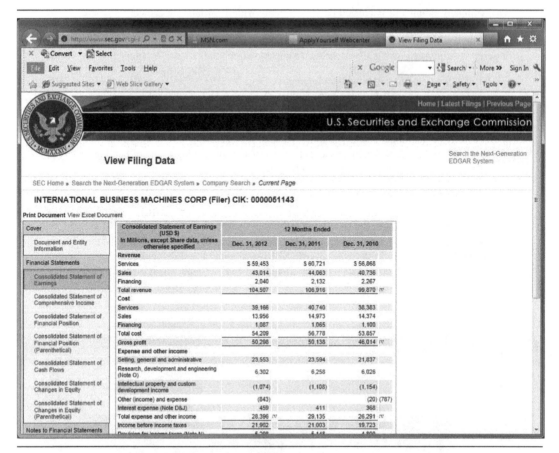

Exhibit 4a.4   IBM's 10-K Consolidated Income Statement (2012-12-31)

determine if it has been properly tagged. Next, notice in the **Details** section that the element's name is **SalesRevenueServicesNet**, it is defined in the **us-gaap** namespace (i.e., the namespace that identifies the standard U.S. GAAP XBRL taxonomy), it is a monetary item with a credit balance, and it is reported for a duration of time. An XML namespace is a convention by which to identify resources available on networks. Each namespace is identified by a preferred prefix (e.g., **us-gaap**) that is appended to the element name in an instance document. Thus, in IBM's instance document, this element will appear as **us-gaap:SalesRevenueServicesNet**, which is translated as "net sales revenues from services as defined in the U.S. GAAP XBRL taxonomy."

Next, close the mini-window for the services revenue line item and notice that each line item through "Gross profit" is a standard U.S. GAAP item; if you click each one and look at its **Details**, you will find that it is defined in the U.S. GAAP XBRL taxonomy. Scroll down to the "Intellectual property and custom development income" line item and *click* it to see its **Definition** and **Details** (see Exhibit 4a.6). What you will discover is that this line item represents a concept unique to IBM and is defined in IBM's extension taxonomy with the element name **IntellectualPropertyAndCustomDevelopmentIncome**, it is a monetary item with a credit balance, and it is reported as of a duration of time. It would appear in IBM's instance document as **ibm:IntellectualPropertyAndCustomDevelopmentIncome**. This is a new (extension) element defined by IBM to represent a concept not found in the standard U.S. GAAP XBRL taxonomy.

Rule number one for all SEC filers is to use elements from the standard U.S. GAAP XBRL taxonomy whenever possible (i.e., if the definition of a concept applies, use the corresponding

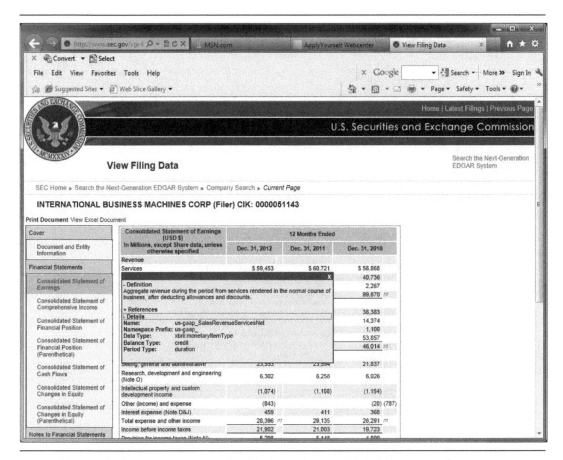

Exhibit 4a.5   IBM's Services Revenue—10-K Consolidated Income Statement (2012-12-31)

element name). Even though the 2012 U.S. GAAP XBRL taxonomy has over 16,000 elements, it cannot contain every conceivable reported concept, and it turns out that there is nothing even close to this concept in the U.S. GAAP XBRL taxonomy. Every extension element that an SEC filer creates should be challenged to determine if an appropriate standard element exists. There are two things that get my attention about this extension item. First, it is a combination of items that are part of IBM's normal operations. A common reason for creating an extension element is a company preferring to report as a single line item a unique combination of otherwise separate concepts. Second, IBM must feel that this item is significant for its financial reporting, as the company has been reporting it for a number of years. The FASB, the official creator and maintainer of the U.S. GAAP taxonomy, and the SEC closely monitor XBRL filings to identify extension elements such as these that might potentially be included in the next release of the taxonomy.

Next, close this mini-window and *click* on IBM's next line item, "Other (income) and expense," and look at its **Definition** and **Details**. IBM defines this extension element as "The aggregate amount of (income) expense, not previously categorized, including interest income, gains and losses on certain derivative instruments, gains and losses from securities and other investments, gains and losses from certain real estate transactions, foreign currency transaction gains and losses, gains and losses from the sale of businesses and amounts related to accretion of asset retirement obligations." IBM's definition is quite detailed, but the concept that it represents, other income and expense, is rather generic. As such, one would think a comparable element would already exist in the standard U.S. GAAP taxonomy. To discover whether it does, point your browser to the XBRL.US website

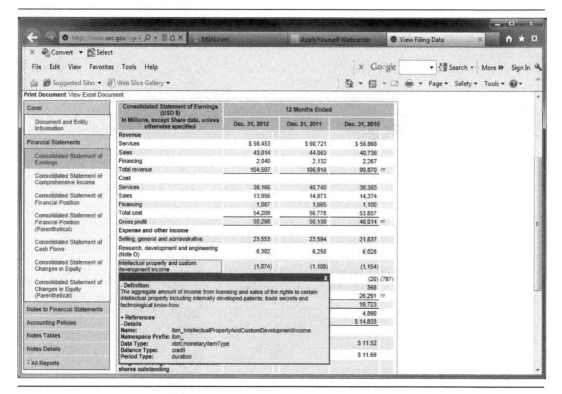

Exhibit 4a.6   IBM's Intellectual Property and Custom Development Income—10-K Consolidated Income Statement (2012-12-31)

http://xbrl.us/Pages/default.aspx and *click* on Taxonomies/SEC Approved Taxonomies/*choose the most recent taxonomy* (2012 as of this writing). Next, *click* the Commercial and Industrial Taxonomy (most companies), and you will load the U.S. GAAP taxonomy viewer (see Exhibit 4a.7).

Next, open Statement of Income (Including Gross Margin) by clicking the + sign in the left-hand margin; continue to open Statement [Line Items] until you find the element "Other Operating Income" (see Exhibit 4a.8). Line items with a red A in a green circle are known as "abstract" items (i.e., they are for organizational purposes and cannot be used as tags), while items with a blue chart represent elements for tagging values in an XBRL instance document.

The left-hand window in the taxonomy viewer contains standard line item labels, and the right-hand window contains three panels with details about a highlighted line item. The Labels panel contains a predefined Standard Label and the Documentation (i.e., definition) for an item. The definition is the first important piece of information to use to help decide if the highlighted item appropriately represents the financial statement concept being reported. Notice that the definition for this item is rather generic but specifically relates to "items that are associated with the entity's normal revenue producing operation." When this definition is compared to that of IBM's "Other (income) and expense" line item, we immediately see that IBM's definition includes gains and losses from many other items, some of which may not be from normal revenue-producing operations. The second important piece of information to use is found in the References panel. If you click the URI (Universal Resource Identifier) link to the FASB's Accounting Standards Codification, you will be asked to register for access to the Codification through either a basic or a professional view. The link will take you to the text of the official Regulation S-X Rule 3-03, Income Statement. This official guidance is often helpful for deciding whether the item is the appropriate one to use. In this case, it lists the various line items that should appear on an income statement and goes on to state that items

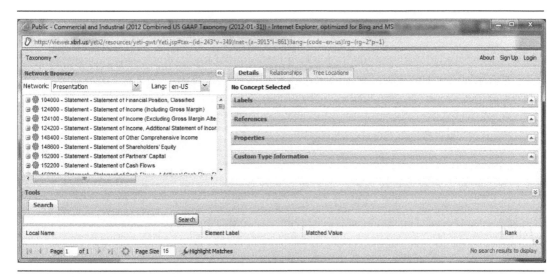

Exhibit 4a.7   The U.S. GAAP Commercial & Industrial Taxonomy Viewer

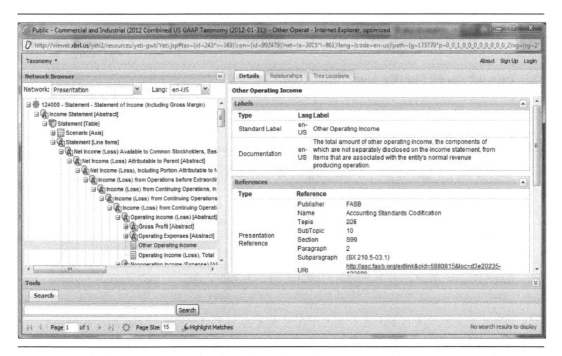

Exhibit 4a.8   The U.S. GAAP Other Operating Income

can be combined if each is less than 10 percent of the total. With these pieces of information, we are gaining confidence that IBM's extension line item may be sufficiently different from the U.S. GAAP item to justify its use.

However, before we reach a conclusion, we need to search the taxonomy to discover if an appropriate item exists somewhere else in the taxonomy. To do so, type *other income and expense* in the taxonomy's search box and scroll down to and *click* the element named **OtherOperating-IncomeExpenseNet** (see Exhibit 4a.9). In reading the definition, you will notice that since it is

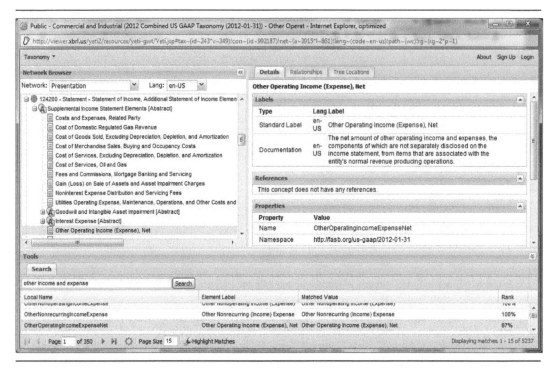

Exhibit 4a.9   The U.S. GAAP Other Operating Income (Expense), Net

a combined income and expense item it is closer to IBM's concept and represents a catchall for other operating income and expenses from normal operations. You will also notice that it does not have an official reference. The items in this part of the taxonomy are classified as "Additional Statement of Income Elements." The majority of these do not have an official reference because they represent a combination of standard income statement items. They are included in the taxonomy because, as mentioned earlier, many companies like to report combined items on the face of their statements. The open question is whether IBM should have used this element as opposed to creating an extension element.

The question is important because extension elements create problems of noncomparability across companies and industries and defeat the smooth operation of analysis tools. One of the basic reasons for creating and mandating reporting in XBRL format is the ability to analyze the contents of financial statements using computerized tools. Extension elements by definition are created by a company to report unique concepts and therefore are not comparable to those of other companies.

Next scroll down to and *click* IBM's "Total expense and other income" line item and look at its **Definition** and **Details**. Once again, IBM has created an extension taxonomy element, **ExpenseAndOtherIncome**, representing a combination of two relatively common financial reporting concepts. If you return to the U.S. GAAP taxonomy, you will find elements named **OperatingEx-penses** and **OtherOperatingIncome** but not the combination. While it is not likely that an analyst or investor would be interested in comparing companies based on "other operating income," the same cannot be said for "total operating expenses," defined in the U.S. GAAP taxonomy as "Generally recurring costs associated with normal operations except for the portion of these expenses which can be clearly related to production and included in cost of sales or services. Includes selling, general and administrative expense." While IBM prefers to report a combined line item, unless disclosed in the notes it is impossible to break out the separate items. This is the reason that analysts currently are using normalized financial data for comparisons across companies and industries, where the detailed data are classified and put into buckets representing standard financial concepts (e.g., total operating expenses).

When preparing XBRL instance documents, every company faces the question of whether to use a predefined U.S. GAAP XBRL element or create an extension element for something that is unique to its way of financial reporting. While it is not the role of standards bodies, such as the FASB, or regulators, such as the SEC, to dictate how a company must tag its line items, creating extension elements for commonly used concepts should be avoided at all costs. This example using IBM's consolidated income statement illustrates two open issues surrounding financial reporting in XBRL format. First, in the future, all companies will have to justify their decision to create an extension element as opposed to using one from the U.S. GAAP XBRL taxonomy. Second, if an extension is justified, should the company be required to create a table showing the differences found in its extension element, including a breakout of elements commonly used by analysts and investors and/or a table reporting all commonly used financial ratios?

Extension taxonomies also include many small changes that do not affect the comparability of financial statements. One such change is the preferred line item labels used by a company on the face of its financials. Each element in the U.S. GAAP taxonomy has a predefined line item label defined in the Labels linkbase. These labels are quite descriptive, and the majority are quite different from those preferred by a company. For example, using the SEC interactive data viewer, *click* IBM's "Income before income taxes" line item and open the **Details** item. You will note that IBM uses the **us-gaap** element **IncomeLossFromContinuingOperationsBefore IncomeTaxesExtraordinaryItemsNoncontrollingInterest** for this item. If you go to the U.S. GAAP XBRL taxonomy, you will find that this element's predefined line item label is "Income (Loss) from Continuing Operations before Equity Method Investments, Income Taxes, Extraordinary Items, Noncontrolling Interest." When IBM created its extension taxonomy, it changed each line item label in the Labels linkbase to its preferred label. Obviously, an extension such as a change to a line item label does not affect the comparability of financial statements or the ability to analyze the reported values.

This brings up another somewhat confusing point about XBRL data files versus the document files we are familiar with. We as humans are used to looking at financial statements as documents in which each line item label is an important piece of information that indicates the meaning of the associated line item value. In XBRL instance documents, however, the most important piece of information is the element name, the tag, from an XBRL taxonomy, because it is meant to be consumed and analyzed by software applications. In other words, labels are for human consumption, but element names, especially those from a nonproprietary, standardized XBRL taxonomy like one of the U.S. GAAP taxonomies, are for use by software applications for analysis, comparison, and reuse.

To conclude this section, each SEC filer creates an XBRL extension taxonomy that includes a subset of the standard U.S. GAAP XBRL taxonomy containing all of the standard XBRL elements used in its instance document and new extension elements created by the company to represent concepts unique to its own reporting. As was mentioned in the Introduction, a company's complete filing in the EDGAR database consists of its document format files, which are its official filings, and its XBRL data files. The XBRL data files include the company's instance document containing each reported value and disclosures tagged with either a standard U.S. GAAP or a company-specific XBRL extension element; the supporting XBRL extension taxonomy consisting of an extension schema; and extension calculation, definition, labels, and presentation linkbases. This is explained in more detail in the next section.

4a.4 XBRL INSTANCE DOCUMENTS

The complete set of XBRL data files is referred to as the instance document and its discoverable taxonomy set (DTS)—referring to an XBRL-enabled software package being able to follow a link from the instance document and validate its contents by "discovering" its taxonomy schema and linkbases. In the EDGAR database, each XBRL data file is named following the SEC's naming convention, including the company's namespace prefix and the end-of-period filing date. In addition, the instance document has an .xml extension, the taxonomy schema has an .xsd extension (standing for XML schema document), and each linkbase includes an abbreviation identifying its type: cal (calculation linkbase), def (definition linkbase), lab (labels linkbase), and pre (presentation linkbase).

An instance document and its DTS are closely connected (see Exhibit 4a.10). Each XBRL instance document is required to have namespaces to support the document's contents, a **schemaRef** element (i.e., "schema reference" element), a **context** element (i.e., "reporting context" element), a **unit** element (i.e., "unit of measure" element), and reported items. Without getting into technical details, namespaces are identifiers that have an assigned prefix and are necessary in all XBRL documents to identify where elements come from. For example, elements from the standard U.S. GAAP taxonomy will have a **us-gaap** prefix (e.g., **us-gaap:GrossProfit**), which differentiates them from company-specific extension elements (e.g., **ibm:ExpenseAndOther-Income**). A **schemaRef** element identifies the location of a company's extension taxonomy schema, which, as explained in the previous section, defines all of the company's extensions to the standard U.S. GAAP taxonomy. A **context** element identifies the company doing the reporting and the period of time that applies, which sets the reporting context. A **unit** element identifies the unit of measure for any and all reported numeric items. Reported items are the facts reported in an XBRL instance document, each tagged with an element from the extension taxonomy or the standard U.S. GAAP taxonomy. A company's XBRL extension schema imports the necessary parts of the U.S. GAAP XBRL schema, other necessary supporting schemas, and references the linkbases that define the details of financial statement calculations, official references, a company's preferred labels, and how items are presented.

XBRL instance documents containing financial statements are quite complex. Point your browser to the SEC company search page at http://sec.gov/edgar/searchedgar/companysearch.html, choose a company (e.g., IBM), click on a "Documents" button next to an "Interactive Data" tag, and then scroll down to the company's data files—its DTS (see Exhibit 4a.11).

The first data file is the company's XBRL instance document containing its reported financial statements, including disclosures; I recommend opening it using the Internet Explorer browser (see Exhibit 4a.12) (more details on browsers later in this section). XBRL instance documents are meant to be consumed by software but follow a strictly defined structure and can be easily understood by humans. The first line in IBM's instance document is an instruction declaring that the document follows the rules for all XML documents and is encoded using US-ASCII (essentially,

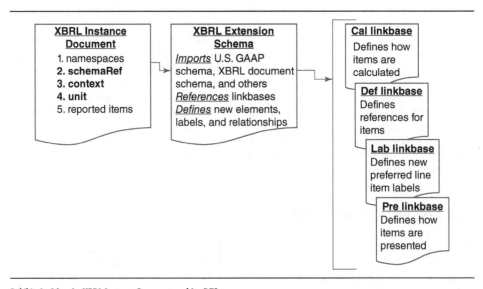

Exhibit 4a.10   An XBRL Instance Document and Its DTS

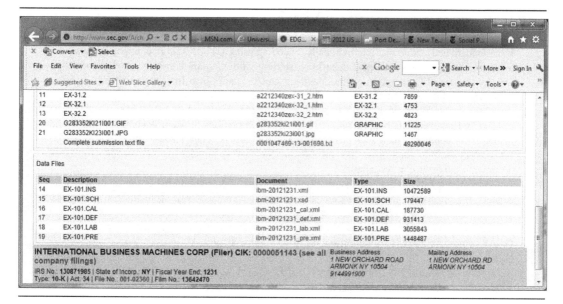

11	EX-31.2	a2212340zex-31_2.htm	EX-31.2	7859
12	EX-32.1	a2212340zex-32_1.htm	EX-32.1	4753
13	EX-32.2	a2212340zex-32_2.htm	EX-32.2	4823
20	G283352KI21I001.GIF	g283352ki21i001.gif	GRAPHIC	11225
21	G283352KI23I001.JPG	g283352ki23i001.jpg	GRAPHIC	1467
	Complete submission text file	0001047469-13-001698.txt		49290046

Data Files

Seq	Description	Document	Type	Size
14	EX-101.INS	ibm-20121231.xml	EX-101.INS	10472589
15	EX-101.SCH	ibm-20121231.xsd	EX-101.SCH	179447
16	EX-101.CAL	ibm-20121231_cal.xml	EX-101.CAL	187730
17	EX-101.DEF	ibm-20121231_def.xml	EX-101.DEF	931413
18	EX-101.LAB	ibm-20121231_lab.xml	EX-101.LAB	3055843
19	EX-101.PRE	ibm-20121231_pre.xml	EX-101.PRE	1448487

INTERNATIONAL BUSINESS MACHINES CORP (Filer) CIK: 0000051143 (see all company filings)
IRS No.: 130871985 | State of Incorp.: NY | Fiscal Year End: 1231
Type: 10-K | Act: 34 | File No.: 001-02360 | Film No.: 13642470

Business Address
1 NEW ORCHARD ROAD
ARMONK NY 10504
9144991900

Mailing Address
1 NEW ORCHARD RD
ARMONK NY 10504

Exhibit 4a.11   IBM's Data Files for Its 10-K 2012-12-31

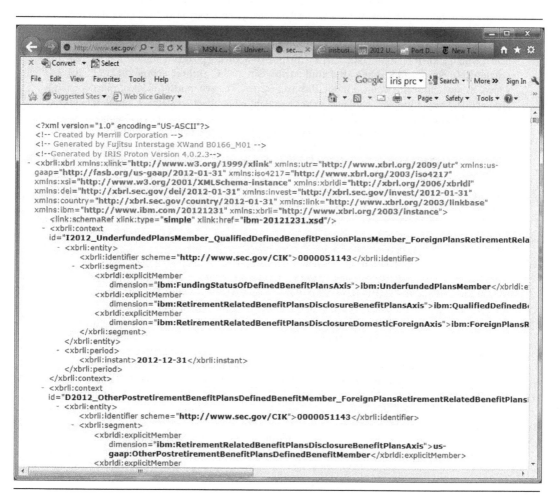

Exhibit 4a.12   IBM's 10-K Instance Document 2012-12-31

U.S. standard text). Note that internationally, encoding using UTF-8 is more common because it is for text in all languages. The next three lines, starting with <!--, are comments or documentation identifying Merrill Corporation as the document creator, the Fujitsu Interstage XWand B0166 as the instance creation software tool, and IRIS Proton as the integration software tool. It may seem surprising that the software giant IBM would outsource the creation of its XBRL instance document to Merrill. However, it is common practice in large corporations to use a document creation and management company, such as Merrill, to create SEC filings. They all now also provide XBRL services. In addition, the Fujitsu XWand software tool is very popular for the creation of instance documents and extension taxonomies.

To explain what you are looking at, the line starting with **<xbrli:xbrl** is the required "root" element for all XBRL instance documents. The root element always contains the namespace declarations that are necessary to support the instance document. Each namespace declaration uses the XML keyword **xmlns**. For example, the following two namespace declarations are for the U.S. GAAP namespace and IBM's namespace identifier for this filing:

1. xmlns:us-gaap="http://fasb.org/us-gaap/2012–01–31"
2. xmlns:ibm="http://www.ibm.com/20121231"

These namespace declarations assign a prefix (e.g., **us-gaap** or **ibm**) and associate it with a URI. The prefixes are then used to identify elements from the U.S. GAAP taxonomy and the IBM extension taxonomy. The other namespace declarations are necessary to support other data found in this instance document.

After the root element, **xbrli:xbrl** (i.e., the element name **xbrl** as defined in the namespace associated with the **xbrli** prefix—**xmlns:xbrli="http://www.xbrl.org/2003/instance"**), is the required **schemaRef** element **<link:schemaRef xlink:type="simple" xlink:href="ibm-20121231.xsd"/>**; which, as you can see, is defined in the **link** namespace. The **schemaRef** element must contain a **type** and an **href** "attribute"; attributes exist to explain more about an element. In the **schemaRef** element, the **xlink:type="simple"** attribute defines a direct link (referred to as a "simple" link), as depicted in Exhibit 4a.10, and the **xlink:href="ibm-20121231.xsd"** attribute identifies the location of IBM's extension taxonomy schema, which is the second item in IBM's SEC EDGAR data files (i.e., **ibm-20121231.xsd**) (see Exhibit 4a.11). After the **schemaRef** element are the **context** elements. Each **context** element must have an **id** attribute, which must start with a letter and be unique in the instance document. The first several **context** elements in IBM's 10-K (Exhibit 4a.12) have long, relatively complex names because they are used to identify members of segments that are reported in IBM's disclosures; these are more complex and will be explained briefly later. For now, *click* the minus sign next to each of these complex **context** elements until you can see IBM's first **context** element with a simple **id** (e.g., **id="D2011"**) (see Exhibit 4a.13).

By convention, most companies' reporting to the SEC includes a date indicator as part of their **context** element **id**. For example, consider IBM's first simple **context** element, **xbrli:context id="D2011"** (Exhibit 4a.13). IBM uses a naming convention in which **D** stands for a *duration* of time, a year (e.g., **2011**). The required **period** element within this **context** element then contains a *start date* and an *end date* element to specifically identify the duration of time that applies (e.g., **<xbrli:startDate>2011-01-01</xbrli:startDate>** and **<xbrli:endDate>2011-12-31</xbrli:endDate>**). Following the same scheme, IBM uses a naming convention in which **I** stands for an *instant* of time—the specific date that identifies the end of the reporting period. Thus, IBM's first *instant* **context** element, **xbrli:context id="I2010"**, contains the **instant** element **<xbrli:instant>2011-12-31</xbrli:instant>**. As you will see, each reported line item has a **contextRef** attribute (meaning context reference) that matches a **context id** and identifies the period of time that applies.

Each **context id** must start with a letter, but the choice of a naming convention is totally up to the company doing the reporting. It is interesting to note that many other companies, including

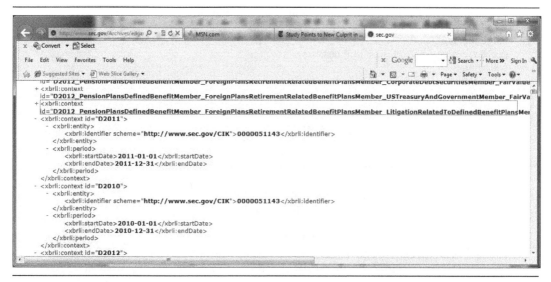

Exhibit 4a.13   IBM's First Simple Context Element—10-K Instance Document 2012-12-31

3M and Hewlett-Packard, have adopted the same easy-to-understand **id** naming convention as IBM. However, naming conventions used in SEC reporting range from easy to understand to quite cryptic:

- GE uses "AS_OF_DEC31_2012"
- Dell uses "I2012Q4"
- Microsoft uses "eol_PE8528——1110-K0015_STD_0_20120720_0"

While GE and Dell use easily understood **context ids**, Microsoft does not. It turns out that Microsoft uses EDGAR Online, Inc. as its XBRL document manager. EDGAR Online uses a sophisticated software package, I-Metrix, and a proprietary naming convention with **context ids** starting with eol document number. In my opinion, as a person who has studied, struggled to understand, and written code to analyze XBRL instance documents, a standardized **context id** naming convention should be mandated. Proprietary naming conventions make it very difficult for a human to understand and a computer application to process and compare the contents of XBRL instance documents.

Each **context id** must be unique in the instance document, because it is used as a reference when reporting items (facts) in an instance document. For example, IBM's gross profit for 2012 is reported as: <**us-gaap:GrossProfit contextRef**="D2012" **unitRef**="USD" **decimals**="-6"> 50298000000</**us-gaap:GrossProfit**>. The **contextRef**="D2012" attribute references the following context element:

<**xbrli:context id**="D2012">
<**xbrli:entity**>
<**xbrli:identifier scheme**="http://www.sec.gov/CIK">0000051143</**xbrli:identifier**>
</**xbrli:entity**>
<**xbrli:period**>
<**xbrli:startDate**>2012-01-01</**xbrli:startDate**>
<**xbrli:endDate**>2012-12-31</**xbrli:endDate**>
</**xbrli:period**>
</**xbrli:context**>

The **unitRef**="USD" attribute references the following **unit** element:

```
<xbrli:unit id="USD">
<xbrli:measure>iso4217:USD</xbrli:measure>
</xbrli:unit>
```

With this context and unit information, a human or a software application can unambiguously interpret this reported fact as: gross profit, as defined in the U.S. GAAP 2012 XBRL taxonomy, in the amount of $50,298,000,000 is being reported by the entity identified by CIK 0000051143 for the period of time 2012-01-01 to 2012-12-31 in U.S. dollars accurate to the nearest million (i.e., the attribute **decimals**="-6" identifies the reported accuracy). Each **context** element identifies the entity doing the reporting and the period of time that applies, and each **unit** element identifies the unit of measure; they are the key to interpreting the fact being reported. Each reported monetary item is required to also have a **decimals** attribute to identify its accuracy.

SEC reporting is very complex, as are the XBRL-formatted financials. IBM's 10-K contains 1,082 **context** elements, including 1,071 for **segment** reporting. Notice IBM's first **context** element shown in Exhibit 4a.12: id="**I2012_UnderfundedPlansMember_QualifiedDefinedBenefit PensionPlansMember_ForeignPlansRetirementRelatedBenefitPlansMember**". The **entity** element contains both an **identifier** element and an optional **segment** element. The **segment** element has three **explicitMember** elements, each identifying an item in separate tables. **Segment** elements are used to identify segments of a company and specific items that appear in tables in a company's footnote disclosures, referred to as "dimensional" reporting. Dimensional reporting is complex and will be covered briefly while discussing Level 4 footnote disclosures.

The reporting of footnote disclosures in XBRL format to the SEC is a mixed bag of the old and the new. It consists of four levels of tagging. All companies in their first year of XBRL reporting to the SEC must tag footnotes at Level 1 and in subsequent years at Levels 1 through 4. Footnote disclosure tagging is best illustrated with an example. Once again, point your browser to the SEC company search page http://sec.gov/edgar/searchedgar/companysearch.html, choose a company (e.g., IBM), and *click* on a "Documents" button next to an "Interactive Data" button; this time *click* the 10-K or 10-Q htm file (typically the first "document format file"), or in the case of IBM *click* the Ex-13 htm file. Then find the "significant accounting policies" footnote disclosure (see Exhibit 4a.14).

Level 1 footnote disclosure tagging requires an entity to tag its entire significant accounting policies and all other significant disclosures as text blocks and preserve the exact formatting as found in the original 10-K or 10-Q document (as in Exhibit 4a.14). In IBM's instance document it appears as in Exhibit 4a.15. Though it looks quite complex, it is simply the text of the disclosures surrounded by the HTML necessary for rendering it in a Web browser. The purpose of Level 1 footnote disclosure tagging is to preserve the exact format of the footnote disclosures so that when it is rendered for human consumption it looks exactly the same.

Notice the element name used for this disclosure, **BasisOfPresentationAndSignificantAccountingPoliciesTextBlock**. Point your browser to the U.S. GAAP 2012 XBRL Commercial and Industrial Taxonomy, scroll down, and open the 195000—Disclosure—Comprehensive Text Block List (see Exhibit 4a.16). There are three types of text blocks for footnote disclosure purposes in the U.S. GAAP taxonomy: Disclosure Text Blocks for Level 1 footnote disclosures, Policy Text Blocks for Level 2, and Table Text Blocks for Level 3. If you open each text block type, you will notice that there are 177 Disclosure Text Block elements, 318 Policy Text Block elements, and 425 Table Text Block elements, each representing a disclosure concept used in U.S. GAAP reporting.

Next, open the Disclosure Text Block [Abstract] item, scroll down, and *click* the **Basis of Presentation and Significant Accounting Policies [Text Block]** line item (see Exhibit 4a.17). Notice its documentation/definition states that it is for the "entire disclosure" of this reporting concept and its properties indicate that it is a "string item" and is reported for a "duration" of time. By definition, all footnote disclosures are *strings* of text and, like income statement and cash flow items, they are reported for a duration of time.

Notice that IBM's Note A: Significant Accounting Policies disclosure (Exhibit 4a.14) contains specific policy disclosures for Basis of Presentation, Principles of Consolidation, Use of Estimates,

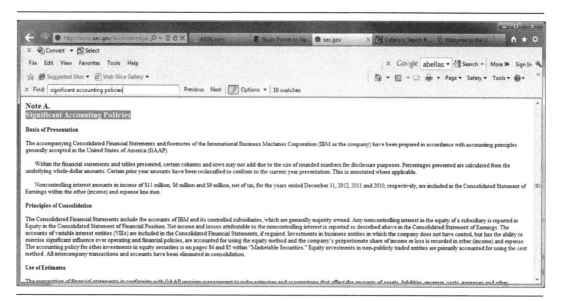

Exhibit 4a.14   IBM's Note A: Significant Accounting Policies in IBM's 10-K Dated 2012-12-31

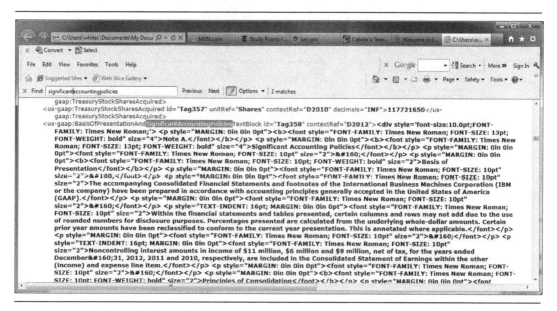

Exhibit 4a.15   IBM's Note A: Significant Accounting Policies Level 1 (Text Block)

Revenue, and so on. For Level 2 disclosure tagging, each has to be tagged with an element representing the specific policy. The majority of policies can be tagged with elements from the U.S. GAAP taxonomy (e.g., **us-gaap:ConsolidationPolicyTextBlock** and **us-gaap:UseOf Estimates**), whereas others are company specific (e.g., **ibm:IntellectualPropertyAndCustom DevelopmentIncomePolicyTextBlock** and **ibm:ProductWarrantiesPolicyTextBlock**). Also note that "PolicyTextBlock" on the end of some of these element names represents a new item type in the 2012 U.S. GAAP

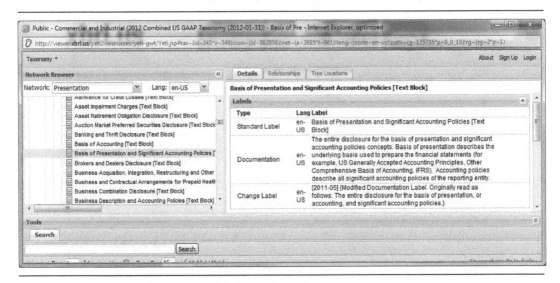

Exhibit 4a.16   U.S. GAAP XBRL Taxonomy Disclosure—Comprehensive Text Block List

Exhibit 4a.17   Basis of Presentation and Significant Accounting Policies [Text Block]

taxonomy; as such, older elements (e.g., **us-gaap:UseOfEstimates**) are still policy elements but retain their original name/type.

Level 1 and Level 2 footnote disclosure tagging requires significant accounting policies to be tagged twice, once as a complete block and then each policy as a specifically identified policy. Footnote disclosures that also contain tables are subject to Level 1 and Level 3 tagging. Consider IBM's Note F (see Exhibit 4a.18). This note is first tagged in its entirety with the element **us-gaap: FinancingReceivablesTextBlock** and then the specific table is tagged in its entirety with the element **us-gaap:ScheduleOfAccountsNotesLoansAndFinancingReceivablesTextBlock**, required for Level 3. Like the new "PolicyTextBlock" elements, the new table text block elements include "TableTextBlock" at the end, whereas older table elements do not.

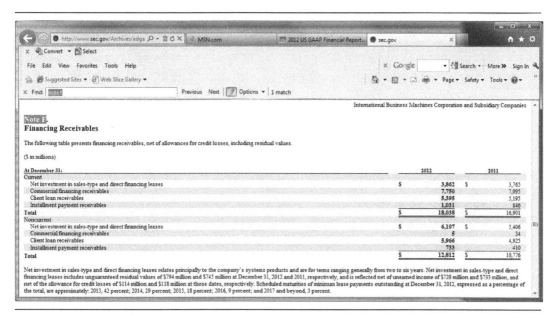

Exhibit 4a.18   IBM's Note F: Financing Receivables Disclosure in IBM's 10-K Dated 2012-12-31

In addition, Level 4 disclosure tagging requires that each individual fact reported in a table or a footnote disclosure be tagged with an appropriate element. Notice the table has a vertical axis that identifies financing receivables by type and a horizontal axis that reports facts by the year that applies. Because of the need to tag individual facts in tables in financial statement disclosures, the U.S. GAAP taxonomy has many predefined tables, axes, domains, and members. Point your browser to the U.S. GAAP 2012 XBRL Commercial and Industrial Taxonomy, scroll down, and *click* the 320000—Disclosure—Receivables, Loans, Notes Receivable, and Others (see Exhibit 4a.19); then *open* the Loans, Notes, Trade and Other Receivables Disclosure [Text Block] and the Accounts, Notes, Loans and Financing Receivable, Gross, Allowance, and Net [Abstract] and keep opening schedules until you can open the Receivable Type [Axis] and the Receivable Type [Domain]; here you will see what are referred to as "domain members." Domain members are abstract items that are used to identify the various components of a concept like current and noncurrent net "accounts, notes, loans and financing receivable." Some are predefined (e.g., loans receivable) and others are unique to a company; in IBM's case the company had to define three abstract domain members: net investment in sales-type and direct financing leases, commercial financing receivables, and installment payment receivables.

This is referred to as "dimensional reporting" and is the most complex part of XBRL financial reporting. Fortunately for the document preparer, the definitions and setup are handled by the software package used to create the XBRL instance document, extension taxonomy, and linkbases.

4a.5 NEW XBRL TAXONOMIES

The U.S. GAAP XBRL taxonomies are updated and improved by the FASB every year on January 31. The URL for the SEC-approved 2013 taxonomy is http://xbrl.fasb.org/us-gaap/2013/elts/us-gaap-std-2013-01-31.xsd. XBRL for financial reporting has been adopted by regulatory bodies, stock exchanges, and governments around the world, and the taxonomies tested and recognized by XBRL International (www.xbrl.org). A sample of these include the Spanish Association of Accounting and Business Administration, the General Purpose Taxonomy of Chinese Accounting Standards, the India Banking GAAP Taxonomy 2010, the Canadian Financial Reporting According to Canadian

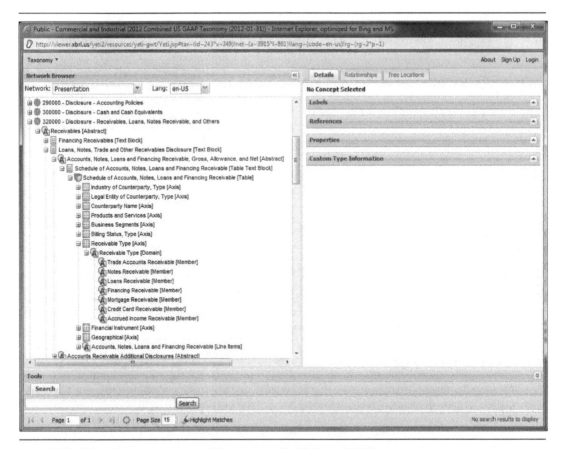

Exhibit 4a.19   Accounts, Notes, Loans, and Financing Receivables Disclosures (2012 Taxonomy)

GAAP, and the Japan EDINET Taxonomy 2010. In addition, newer XBRL taxonomies have been recognized and released for a number of different domains, including the U.S. Governance, Risk and Compliance (GRC) Taxonomy (2010) and the U.S. Corporate Actions Taxonomy (2012). The GRC taxonomy is designed for use by domestically registered investment management firms to file SEC Form N-PX for recording proxy investor votes. The 2012 Corporate Actions Taxonomy is designed to "electronically connect the issuer and investor" (XBRL.US) by providing a global standard with which to ensure that the "issuers' intention and information are accurately and effectively delivered" to investors. Currently there are an estimated "200,000 corporate actions such as dividends, bond redemptions, and mergers" announced each year by publicly traded companies, and most of the information is manually processed, entered, and reentered into computerized documents (XBRL.US). The Corporate Actions Taxonomy is designed to standardize the terminology and the computerized processing of corporate actions information, thereby reducing errors and miscommunication and streamlining the communication process. With these newer taxonomies for registering proxy votes and documenting and communicating corporate actions, XBRL taxonomies are being developed for broader, nonfinancial applications. It is on its way to becoming a standard for improving business communications and financial and nonfinancial business processes.

4a.6 SUMMARY

As you likely realize from this introduction, XBRL reporting in the SEC EDGAR database is quite complex. The EDGAR database contains the document format files that are the original SEC filings and exhibits, along with the data files that are the XBRL financials, extension taxonomy schema, and linkbases; together they are the XBRL discoverable taxonomy set (DTS). The SEC interactive data viewing tool is valuable for helping to understand the connection between the humanly readable financial statements we are familiar with and the XBRL element name and definition behind each reported item. The XBRL instance document containing the reported financial facts and disclosures is itself quite complex, and its supporting extension schema and linkbases are even more complex. Fortunately, most of this complexity is handled by software tools used to create the instance documents and extension taxonomies, including Fujitsu XWand, EDGAR Online I-Metrix, and Rivet Crossfire. At the present time, most companies use their tried-and-true, and often onerous, financial reporting processes to collect, aggregate, and create their quarterly and annual financial reports to the SEC and then add on the required XBRL reporting. Most experts agree that in the future, as tools become more sophisticated, the XBRL documents will be the originals from which the humanly readable documents will be created. The end result will be more efficient reporting processes, lower costs, more usable data, and greater transparency.

In the meantime, there are a few issues identified in this chapter and a number of others that are emerging as necessary for seeing XBRL deliver on its promise of decreasing the burden and costs of financial reporting to companies and regulators, improving the accuracy and timeliness of the reported data, and improving the usefulness and usability of the reported data to investors and analysts. First, in its current form the SEC mandate for XBRL reporting is increasing, not decreasing, the burden and costs of financial reporting to publicly traded companies. Most companies are paying their SEC document manager/publisher additional fees to do the XBRL tagging and validation. Those companies that are doing it in-house have formed a group of specialists to do the work. As such groups gain experience with the process, costs should go down. However, until the XBRL tagging becomes an integral part of the accounting and financial reporting processes and businesses begin to leverage it for additional reporting requirements, it will continue to be an additional step and expense in the reporting process. Second, XBRL financials are not audited. Currently, there is a set of assurance guidelines, AICPA SOP 09-01 (American Institute of Certified Public Accountants, 2009), but no audit framework. As implemented by the SEC, companies have two years of limited liability for their XBRL financials; this means that all of the first phase of filers, the 500 largest companies reporting under U.S. GAAP that began XBRL reporting in 2009, no longer have limited liability for their XBRL financials. Though the data are not public, the largest accounting firms have developed XBRL assurance practices, and many large companies are paying for such services. And in 2012, the AICPA has developed a set of Principles and Criteria for XBRL-Formatted Information. Until the future, when XBRL tagging becomes an integral part of business processes such that a company's financial statements can be generated from XBRL source data and auditors are auditing the end result, this will continue to be an issue. Third, XBRL instance documents and their associated extension schemas and linkbases in the EDGAR database are quite difficult to use and analyze. The data/reported facts in XBRL instance documents are tagged in such a way as to be unambiguously interpretable by a human or software application, but the complexity of doing so is great. A human has to have a deep knowledge of XBRL, commercial software applications are complex and often expensive, and the complexity of XBRL tagging and U.S. GAAP reporting complicates automated analysis processes. Some of the suggestions mentioned in this chapter, such as standard context ids and a table of extension elements and standard ratios, would improve transparency and help alleviate the usability problem.

In conclusion, though XBRL is now in use around the world, it is still an emerging technology. XBRL reporting, the software tools for the creation and analysis of XBRL documents, and the specification itself will continue to evolve and improve. A recent example is the emergence of a new approach to XBRL known as iXBRL ("inline" XBRL), a relatively new specification that embeds an XBRL instance document within an XHTML document. iXBRL combines the XBRL instance document with XHTML so that a Web browser displays it in a humanly readable form, essentially making the XBRL tagged data the source for the financial statements as opposed to a separate document as in SEC reporting. iXBRL is now mandated for companies reporting to the HM Revenue and Customs House in the United Kingdom. This also illustrates that XBRL is a moving target, creating an additional problem for XBRL users, analysts, and software developers.

In any case, I hope this introduction to XBRL and reporting in the EDGAR database has helped your understanding of financial statements in XBRL format. In an informative article and case study about SEC XBRL compliance, John Stantial, Director of Financial Reporting at United Technologies Corporation, writes about the current and future benefits of building an in-house team and integrating XBRL tagging within a company's reporting processes (*Journal of Accountancy*, 2007). I recommend it as food for thought for going forward with XBRL reporting. For an in-depth understanding of XBRL and the underlying XML and supporting technologies, see *The Accountant's Guide to XBRL* (7th edition) (January 2013).

4a.7 REFERENCES

American Institute of Certified Public Accountants. *SOP 09-1, Performing Agreed-Upon Procedures Engagements That Address the Completeness, Accuracy, or Consistency of XBRL-Tagged Data*. New York, April 2009.

Assurance Services Executive Committee. *Principles and Criteria for XBRL-Formatted Information*. New York, 2012.

EDGAR Online I-Metrix, http://i-metrix.edgar-online.com.

Fujitsu Interstage XWand, www.fujitsu.com/global/services/software/interstage/solutions/xbrl.

Rivet Crossfire, www.rivetsoftware.com/products/crossfire/default.aspx.

Stantial, John. "ROI on XBRL". *Journal of Accountancy*, June 1, 2007.

White, Clinton. *The Accountant's Guide to XBRL*, 7th ed., January 2013, www.skipwhite.com.

CHAPTER 7

INTRODUCTION TO INTERNAL CONTROL ASSESSMENT AND REPORTING (ADDENDUM)

Lynford Graham, CPA, PhD, CFE
Bentley University

7.10 2012 JOBS ACT

In 2012, Congress passed the Jumpstart our Business Startups (JOBS) Act.[1] For new start-up (emerging growth) companies registered after the effective date of the Act, there is an effective five-year waiver of the provisions of Section 404(b)—the auditor attestation regarding entity internal controls effectiveness. Under prior regulation there was a two-year phase-in for newly registered companies to come under Section 404 requirements. The JOBS Act extended that phase-in three more years. To qualify as an emerging growth company, revenues of the new entity should be less than $1 billion (under U.S. generally accepted accounting principles [GAAP]). Some entities in this category would have qualified as accelerated filers under existing regulations (e.g., capitalization of $75 million or more). Note that this provision applies only to the 404(b) provision of the Sarbanes-Oxley Act (SOX). Managements must still assess, test, and report on the effectiveness of their internal controls, as before. A series of helpful questions and answers regarding the Act is posted on the Securities and Exchange Commission (SEC) website at www.sec.gov/divisions/corpfin/guidance/cfjjobsactfaq-title-i-general.htm.

7.11 2013 REVISION OF THE COSO INTERNAL CONTROL—INTEGRATED FRAMEWORK

Since the Sarbanes-Oxley Act was passed in 2002, the principal benchmark framework used in standard setting and regulation for entity and auditor assessment of the effectiveness of internal controls has been the 1992 *Internal Control—Integrated Framework* by the Committee of Sponsoring Organizations (COSO). In 2006 COSO published a version of the framework designed to assist smaller public entities in implementing the COSO framework, and in 2009 COSO published additional guidance on the monitoring component.

On May 14, 2013, COSO released a multiple-volume revision of the COSO framework. After December 15, 2014, the existing framework and subsequent guidance will be considered superseded

---

[1] www.gpo.gov/fdsys/pkg/BILLS-112hr3606enr/pdf/BILLS-112hr3606enr.pdf.

by the new framework. The new framework retains the same five main components as in the 1992 and 1996 guidance, but identifies 17 principles that underlie these components. While still conceptual in nature, the new volumes provide sample templates for documentation as well as approaches and examples to help users identify how the principles can be met, documented, and tested. To consider internal controls to be effective, COSO indicates that three criteria should be met: (1) the five components should be satisfied, (2) the 17 principles should be satisfied, and (3) the system of internal controls should be applied in an integrated way.

Regulators and standard setters may respond to the new guidance. Entities should be alert for new regulator guidance regarding these changes. Entities will need to assess how the new requirements compare to their current practices and identify whether changes are desirable or necessary. Those users closely following the 2006 COSO guidance will find the 20 principles from that guidance similar to the new requirements. There are two new principles introduced, and five of the 2006 principles have been merged into the current 17.

The revised COSO guidance can be ordered from the American Institute of Certified Public Accountants (AICPA) at www.CPA2biz.com.

IMPLEMENTING THE BALANCED SCORECARD (NEW)

Les Livingstone, MBA, PhD, CPA (NY & TX)
University of Maryland, University College

10a.1 INTRODUCTION AND BACKGROUND

As a former financial executive in several large organizations, the author has learned that the financial statements are widely used for evaluating both the performance of the organization and also that of its management. Why do we distinguish between the performance of the organization, on the one hand, and the performance of its management, on the other hand? One reason is that the performance of the organization may be mediocre—for example, if the organization is in a depressed industry. But at the same time the performance of management might be very good if management is able to obtain results that surpass the average in that depressed industry, even if those results are objectively second-rate when compared with the results of organizations in thriving industries. In other words, organization performance might be evaluated in an absolute manner, in comparison with the performance of all organizations, regardless of whether the subject organization happens to be in an economic sector that is depressed or in one that is thriving. But the performance of management might be appraised in a relative manner, taking into account the economic prosperity (or lack thereof) prevailing in its sector of the economy.

Of course, performance evaluation is significant, whether done internally, within the organization (for example, by the board of directors) or externally, outside the organization (for example, by investors). Certainly performance evaluation is important and necessary. But there are problems attached to conventional performance evaluation, based on financial statement information. One major problem is that financial statements are historical in nature, and consequently backward-looking. Therefore, using financial statements for performance evaluation is like driving an automobile by using only the rearview mirror, and not looking ahead through the windshield. It follows that too much time may elapse at times when faster action is necessary to correct a matter that has caused damage to the organization, and to get back on the right course.

In summary, performance evaluation may take place in various contexts, as summarized in Exhibit 10a.1.

As shown in the exhibit, performance evaluation may be done inside of the organization (cell 1) or outside of the organization (cell 3) or inside of the management (cell 2) or outside of the management (cell 4). In addition, the evaluation of performance may use trailing or "after the fact" information, or the evaluation of performance may use predictive or "before the fact" data.

(a) LAGGING OR LEADING INDICATORS.   A recent article states that "finance teams have long been tasked with gazing into the past. They were the ones with answers about how the company has performed over time, how it did in the past month, and how it just did compared with how it used to do. But now finance professionals are being asked to turn the time machine around, using their skills to guide companies into the future."[1] Economists refer to this issue as using lagging indicators (which tend to be after the fact and therefore slow) rather than leading indicators (which tend to predict problems in advance, instead of being after the fact, and are therefore fast). Many attempts have been made to move from lagging indicators to leading indicators. As one example, I was budget director for a 500-store retail chain, and we relied on monthly financial statements for regular performance evaluation. The monthly financial statements were produced as a rule around 10 days after the end of each month, and this was considered quite reasonably fast. However, whenever there was a problem, it would take about 10 more days to investigate it and to get it resolved. As a result, it took about 10 days to produce the monthly financial statements, plus another 10 days to solve any problems—making a total of 20 days until emerging problems could be put to rest. Actually, it was only problems arising on the last day of the month that needed only 20 days to resolve.

A little more thought reveals that problems could arise on any day of the month. With an average of 30 days in any month of the year, problems can be thought of as arising on average around the middle of the month—say the 15th of the month. That would add another 15 days to the previous total of 20 days for the delay in solving a typical problem. All in all, then the typical problem took 35 (20 + 15 = 35) days from origin to resolution, and thus 35 days meant a delay of more than a month. And what were the causes of these typical problems in the 500-store retail chain? The causes most often seen were unauthorized markdowns, inventory shrinkage beyond the customary 1 percent, unnecessary hiring of temporary staff, stockouts of necessary ("never out") items, merchandise shortages, or unexpected expenses (such as weather damage to store premises, accidents like customer slips or falls beyond the norm, and uninsured burglary losses). Laboring under the weight of an average delay

Performance Evaluation	Organization Performance	Management Performance
Internal Evaluation	1	2
External Evaluation	3	4

Exhibit 10a.1   Modes of Performance Evaluation

[1] "Flexing the Strategy Muscles," *Journal of Accountancy*, April 2013.

of more than a month of undetected and unsolved problems laid a penalty of lost profits upon the organization. This penalty provided an incentive to produce the monthly financial statements more promptly than the customary 10th of each following month.

After several months of trial and error, we were able to produce the monthly financial statements more promptly than the customary 10th of each following month. Various techniques were tried out, and some that proved to be effective were these:

- We required all store managers to get advance permission from our office before hiring temporary staff.
- We required all department heads and executives to obtain prior authorization before issuing purchase orders for any expenditure, and no expenditures were permitted without a purchase order.
- We requested that our office be informed as early as possible about any markdowns, inventory shrinkage beyond the customary 1 percent, stockouts of necessary ("never out") items, merchandise shortages, or unexpected expenses (such as weather damage to store premises, accidents like customer slips or falls beyond the norm, and uninsured burglary losses).

Due to the success of these techniques, we were eventually able to produce monthly for performance pro forma (predicted) financial statements by the 20th of the very same month. These monthly pro forma financial statements were—after a year—able to predict the actual monthly financial statements within about 5 percent. In effect, we had derived a set of leading indicators to supplement the traditional lagging indicators represented by the actual monthly financial statements. That helped to solve one of the problems relating to the use of financial statements for performance evaluation—namely, that historical financial statements contain lagging indicators rather than leading indicators of performance.

Exhibit 10a.2 shows the combined effects of internal and external evaluations of both organization and management performance, based either on lagging or on leading indicators of performance. More specifically, there are eight different aspects of performance evaluation that are displayed in Exhibit 10a.2, as follows:

1. Internal evaluation of organization performance, using lagging indicators
2. Internal evaluation of organization performance, using leading indicators
3. Internal evaluation of management performance, using lagging indicators
4. Internal evaluation of management performance, using leading indicators
5. External evaluation of organization performance, using lagging indicators
6. External evaluation of organization performance, using leading indicators
7. External evaluation of management performance, using lagging indicators
8. External evaluation of management performance, using leading indicators

While it is useful to be able to solve one set of organizational problems, there is also another problem, which is the difficulty that plagues organizations in the implementation of organizational strategy.

Performance Evaluation	Organization Performance	Management Performance
Internal Evaluation	1 Lagging	3 Lagging
	2 Leading	4 Leading
External Evaluation	5 Lagging	7 Lagging
	6 Leading	8 Leading

Exhibit 10a.2   Lagging and Leading Modes of Performance Evaluation

10a.2 THE PROBLEM OF IMPLEMENTING STRATEGY

Over the past 10 years, two-thirds of incidents due to strategy missteps caused declines of 50 percent or more in corporate stock prices, according to chief auditors listing strategy implementation as a top concern.[2] Strategy was also the top priority for improvement cited by North American CFOs.[3] As a former principal in a prominent international consulting firm, the author has participated in many strategy assignments for leading organizations of a for-profit and a not-for-profit nature. From these assignments it has become clear that most large organizations tend to have well-thought-out strategic plans. But most large organizations share similar challenges to their strategies. These major challenges are:

- Most large organizations have excellent strategic plans. But they have great difficulty in successfully implementing their strategies—no matter how well thought out their strategic plans happen to be.
- Most seasoned consultants would readily agree that a second-rate strategy with first-rate implementation is preferable to a first-rate strategy with second-rate implementation.
- Further, organizational personnel often do not understand how metrics of their regular everyday activities contribute to the overall goals and strategy of the entire organization. If you ask many organization employees how their daily tasks contribute to the attainment of organization strategic objectives, you are likely to see only blank stares and hear only puzzled responses of "I don't know" or "I have no idea."

The technique that best overcomes these challenges is the Balanced Scorecard.

10a.3 THE BALANCED SCORECARD

The Balanced Scorecard is widely used in business and industry, government, and not-for-profit organizations worldwide to align operating activities to the vision and strategy of the organization and to monitor organization performance against strategic goals. It was originated by Dr. Robert Kaplan of the Harvard Business School and David Norton as a performance measurement framework that adds strategic nonfinancial performance measures to traditional financial metrics to give managers and executives a more balanced view of organizational performance.

The Balanced Scorecard has these remarkable advantages:

- It links the regular everyday activities of each organizational unit to the overall organization strategy.
- It enables organizational personnel to understand how metrics of their regular everyday activities contribute to the overall goals and strategy of the entire organization.
- It tracks the performance of each organization unit, and by this means it monitors progress in the implementation of organization strategy for each organization unit.
- It supplements the traditional financial performance measures with nonfinancial performance measures, which allow forward-looking indicators to be added to the backward-looking traditional financial performance metrics.

---

[2] According to a corporate executive board cited in the article "Flexing the Strategy Muscles" in the *Journal of Accountancy*, April 2013.

[3] According to a recent Deloitte survey noted in the article "Flexing the Strategy Muscles" in the *Journal of Accountancy*, April 2013.

Performance Evaluation	Organization Performance	Management Performance
Internal Evaluation	1 Lagging 2 Leading	3 Lagging 4 Leading

Exhibit 10a.3   Lagging and Leading Modes of Internal Performance Evaluation

The Balanced Scorecard is the most widely used system of performance management. For example, the U.K. Cranfield University found that 75 percent of organizations with formal performance management systems use a system based on the Balanced Scorecard.[4] The Balanced Scorecard has become the leading system for managing organizational performance, outdistancing systems based on quality management (such as Six Sigma).[5]

The Balanced Scorecard is essentially a system for effective implementation of organization strategy. As a rule, the Balanced Scorecard is strictly an internal system, and is not made available externally outside the organization to investors or suppliers or customers or other external groups. The reason for this is that each organization unit has its own specially tailored Balanced Scorecard, and therefore the Balanced Scorecard system in most cases is very elaborate and extremely ponderous—which makes it far too cumbersome and too massive for external use. Accordingly, this fact of internal use reduces the scope of the Balanced Scorecard system by eliminating its use externally. So Exhibit 10a.2 no longer requires external performance evaluation, and thus shrinks down to the table shown in Exhibit 10a.3.

Exhibit 10a.3 requires only half of the performance evaluations of Exhibit 10a.2, by virtue of eliminating external performance evaluations. But use of the Balanced Scorecard system does require a unique and distinctive Balanced Scorecard for each organization unit. While it may seem paradoxical, each organization unit has a unique and distinctive Balanced Scorecard, but—at the same time—the Balanced Scorecards for all organization units need to be in mutual harmony with one another, and to be totally consistent with the overall strategy of the entire organization. A good analogy is the typical symphony orchestra where each instrumental section has its own unique sound; for example, the violin section sounds quite different from the brass section, which sounds quite different from the woodwinds, which in turn differ radically from the percussion section, and so on. Yet, despite their very different sound qualities, all instrumental sections play the same piece of music at the same time, in harmony with each other.

What are the different objectives—in addition to the lagging indicators in the traditional financial statements?

(a) THE LEADING INDICATORS. By analyzing current perspectives as well as the historical financial metrics, managers can better translate the organization's strategy into actionable objectives and more quickly measure how well or otherwise the strategic plan is being implemented. In addition to the financial perspective, these current perspectives are typically:

- The customer perspective
- The internal processes perspective
- The organizational learning and growth perspective

In order to start development of a Balanced Scorecard, organizations usually appoint a task force to get the ball rolling. The task force's mission is to develop a first draft of the objectives and metrics for the Balanced Scorecard. More specifically, for the entire organization, the task force will designate at least three objectives per perspective for the three perspectives listed. Each objective should be reflected by a metric, which measures the extent to which that objective is being accomplished.

---

[4] "Flexing the Strategy Muscles."
[5] According to a corporate executive board cited in the article "Flexing the Strategy Muscles."

(b) CHARACTERISTICS OF METRICS.   Numbers are the language of purposeful activity. Numbers are measurements of performance for organizations and for organizational units. These performance measurements determine whether organizations or organizational units are succeeding or failing in reaching their objectives. If the measurements are favorable, then organizations are succeeding, employees are earning increased compensation and greater job security, customers are pleased, suppliers are winning more orders, the local community is benefiting, and investors are earning good returns. However, if the measurements are unfavorable, then organizations are not succeeding, employees are earning only constant or reduced compensation and losing job security, customers are displeased, suppliers are winning fewer orders, the local community is being harmed, and investors are earning low or even negative returns. Therefore performance measurement numbers are of crucial importance. These performance measurement numbers are known as metrics.

It is very important to understand what a metric is. To be clear, a metric means a measurement. There are three kinds of measurements:

1. *Nominal:* A nominal scale assigns items to a category. The category may be a simple "yes" or "no." For example, "yes" or "no" categories can be red or yellow, male or female, or odd or even. In the case of a family, a nominal scale assigns items to categories like grandfather, grandmother, father, mother, son, or daughter. In the case of an automobile, categories could be small sedan, midsize sedan, large sedan, SUV, and so on.

2. *Ordinal:* An ordinal scale identifies items only in their order of magnitude. For example, a customer survey might ask for ratings of service on a scale of 1 through 5, where 5 is best and 1 is worst. That means a score of 4 is better than a score of 2. But it does not mean that a 4 is twice as good as a 2, or that a 4 is four times as good as a 1.

3. *Cardinal:* A cardinal scale is also known as a ratio scale. For example, the numbers 1, 2, 3, 4, 5, and so on represent a cardinal scale. For a cardinal or ratio scale, 12 is 6 times 2, and 4 times 3, and 3 times 4, and 2 times 6.

So a metric must be either a nominal, ordinal, or cardinal measurement. Anything else is not a metric. For example:

- ROE >20% is a metric.
- "Increase sales revenue by 5 percent" is a metric.
- "Collect 95 percent of receivables within 30 days" is a metric.
- "Survey customers" is not a metric.
- "Adhere to written policies" is not a metric.

For each metric in each period there are (1) target values, (2) actual values, and (3) a methodology for obtaining the data and calculating the actual values.

The Balanced Scorecard normally contains four perspectives:

1. *Financial perspective:* financial statement measures for objectives such as liquidity, solvency, and return on invested capital

2. *Customer perspective:* metrics for objectives like customer loyalty, customer growth, and customer satisfaction

3. *Internal process perspective:* metrics for objectives such as policies, procedures, and technologies used

4. *Organizational learning and growth perspective:* metrics for objectives such as employee training and development, innovation, and skills

For each perspective, there are usually three metrics. Each metric is reported both as the actual result and the target value, so that the actual result can easily be compared with the target value. The concept is to keep the objectives down to a few major concerns in order to focus on essentials, and not

Perspective	Objectives	Metrics	Target Value	Actual Value
Financial	3	3	3	3
Customer	3	3	3	3
Internal	3	3	3	3
Learning	3	3	3	3

Exhibit 10a.4   Balanced Scorecard Perspectives, Objectives, and Metrics

Perspective	Objective	Metric	Target Value
Financial	Tuition revenue	Annual rate of growth	>6%
	Operating surplus	% Operating surplus growth	>7%
	Solvency	Ratio of total assets to total liabilities	>2.0
Customer	Increase student enrollment	Annual rate of student increase	2%
	Maintain tuition per credit hour	Average tuition per credit	$600
	Improve satisfaction	Median score: student survey	>90%
Internal	Improve technology	% Information technology (IT) expense to revenue	>4%
	More powerful but more user-friendly software	Ratio of new to old software products	>8%
	Maintain market share	Market share %	>24%
Learning	Employee training	Annual hours of training per employee	30
	Employee turnover	Employee turnover	<3%
	Employee pay	Average compensation per employee	$38,000 +

Exhibit 10a.5   Sample Metrics for a Small College

to be distracted by items of lesser importance. Often the analogy is used of an automobile dashboard, which contains only the major factors, such as fuel level, speed, mileage, engine temperature, and various warning lights in case of malfunctioning components.

Exhibit 10a.4 shows the basic balanced scorecard framework.

It is probably useful at this stage to describe a practical application of the Balanced Scorecard. Exhibit 10a.5 presents an example for a small liberal arts college. This example deals only with the Balanced Scorecard for the college as a whole, and not with the Balanced Scorecard for any of the individual organizational units within the college.

This example contains the customary four perspectives, and each perspective has within itself three objectives. For each of these three objectives, there is an actual metric plus a target value for that metric.

10a.4 THE BALANCED SCORECARD PROCESS

The rough draft Balanced Scorecard shown in the preceding section is simply a first step in a lengthy ongoing process. This rough draft Balanced Scorecard still needs considerable thought and discussion in order to make it into an effective means to implement strategy and to measure organizational performance in attaining the related strategic objectives. For example, it needs to be decided whether the three stated objectives listed for each perspective are the best choices that should be made. A great deal of analysis and discussion is probably required before this issue can be settled. After that issue has been agreed, the next step is to find suitable metrics for each objective. That step too will require careful analysis and discussion.

After the metrics have finally been determined, their target values will need to be set. It is important that these target values are challenging so that the organization will need to put forth effort and initiative in order to achieve the targets. At the same time, the targets should not be so difficult that they are virtually impossible to achieve, because that would induce people to fling up their arms in despair and simply give up trying to do the impossible. So a delicate sense of balance is necessary in setting the target values of the metrics. The target values have to be challenging on the one hand, but not so challenging as to be impossible on the other hand.

Once the college Balanced Scorecard has finally been determined, it is the mutually agreed master Balanced Scorecard for the top executive group of the college. The next step in the process is to cascade Balanced Scorecards down to each organizational unit of the college. Each faculty department should have its own Balanced Scorecard. For example, there will be one for the English department, one for the chemistry department, one for the mathematics department, one for the political science department, and so on. Also, each administrative department of the college will need its own individual Balanced Scorecard. There will be one for Student Recruiting, one for Student Advising, one for the Finance Department, one for Student Financial Aid, and so on. There will also be Balanced Scorecards for support and service departments, such as Buildings and Grounds, Maintenance, and Security.

Clearly the initial efforts will demand many staff meetings, much staff training, and a great deal of support and supervision, and coordination so that the work proceeds as planned, on time and on budget. It is important that each organization design and construct its own Balanced Scorecard in order to build ownership, enthusiasm, and personal involvement in the Balanced Scorecard project. Of course, the Balanced Scorecard for each unit should require approval from the college executive under which it operates.

But any changes made to secure that approval should be suggested or requested, rather than being ordered or imposed by authority. This is very important, so that each organization unit retains ownership, enthusiasm, and personal involvement in its own Balanced Scorecard, and also for the entire Balanced Scorecard project as a whole.

Next we introduce rough, preliminary Balanced Scorecards for the following:

- One representative academic department
- One representative administrative department
- One representative support and service department

Note that most Balanced Scorecards for academic departments are likely to be quite similar to one another. For example, the Balanced Scorecard for the history department is likely to resemble the Balanced Scorecard for the statistics department, which in turn is likely to look a lot like the Balanced Scorecard for the psychology department. Given that all Balanced Scorecards for academic departments are likely to be quite similar to one another, it is satisfactory to save the reader from needless duplication by presenting just one generic (sample) Balanced Scorecard to represent all Balanced Scorecards for academic departments.

By the same token, we will save the reader from needless duplication by presenting just one Balanced Scorecard to represent all administrative departments, and also just one Balanced Scorecard to represent all support and service departments. We continue first with one representative academic department.

In Exhibit 10a.6 note the following important points:

- See how the metrics for an academic department (in Exhibit 10a.6) differ from the metrics for the entire college (in Exhibit 10a.5).
- Also note the compatibility between the metrics for an academic department (in Exhibit 10a.6) and the metrics for the entire college (in Exhibit 10a.5).
- On the one hand, there is necessarily a difference between the Balanced Scorecards for the entire college and for an academic department. On the other hand, there is necessarily compatibility between the Balanced Scorecards for the entire college and for an academic department.
- There is an alignment in the Balanced Scorecard between traditional performance measurement (the financial perspective) and the remaining metrics (the other three perspectives).

Perspective	Objective	Metric	Target Value
Financial	Department tuition revenue	Annual rate of growth	>6%
	Department expense budget	% Growth	<5%
	Department capital expenditures	Purchases of equipment	<$25,000
Customer	Department student body	Annual rate of student increase	2%
	Maintain tuition per credit hour	Average tuition per credit	$600
	Improve student satisfaction	Median score: student survey	>90%
Internal	Improve technology	% IT expense to revenue	>4%
	More powerful software	Ratio of new to old software products	>8%
	Maintain market share	Market share %	>22%
Learning	Employee training	30	
	Employee turnover	<3%	
	Employee pay	$38,000 +	

Exhibit 10a.6   Sample Metrics for an Academic Department

(a) A SAMPLE BALANCED SCORECARD FOR AN ADMINISTRATIVE DEPARTMENT. In a liberal arts college there are likely to be a number of administrative departments, such as Student Recruiting, Faculty and Staff Recruiting, Student Advising, Financial Aid, Legal, and Information Technology (IT), to name a few. Typically, administrative departments have no revenue, but do have costs. Like the academic departments, the administrative departments will also differ individually, but will also share many similar characteristics. Therefore, as in the case of an academic department, we can also visualize a generic administrative department. The administrative department is represented by the Balanced Scorecard in Exhibit 10a.7.

In Exhibit 10a.7 note the following important points:

- See how the metrics for an administrative department (in Exhibit 10a.7) differ from the metrics for the entire college (in Exhibit 10a.5).
- Also note the compatibility between the metrics for the administrative department (in Exhibit 10a.7) and the metrics for the entire college (in Exhibit 10a.5).
- On the one hand, there is necessarily a difference between the Balanced Scorecards for the entire college and for the administrative department. On the other hand, there is necessarily

Perspective	Objective	Metric	Target Value
Financial	Department total cost	Annual rate of growth	<5%
	Department salary budget	% Growth	<5%
	Department capital expenditures	Purchases of equipment	<$20,000
Customer	Maintain response time	Average time to respond	<1 day
	Improve client[a] satisfaction	Median score: client survey	>90%
	Quality of service	Demonstrate quality of service by competitive bid	Win all bids
Internal	Improve technology	% IT expense to revenue	>4%
	More powerful software	Ratio of new to old software products	>8%
	Avoid complaints	Ratio of complaints to compliments	<10%
Learning	Employee training	Annual hours of employee training	30
	Employee turnover	Employee turnover	<3%
	Employee pay	Average employee compensation	$32,000

[a] Clients of college administrative departments tend to be other organization units in the same college.

Exhibit 10a.7   Sample Metrics for an Administrative Department

compatibility between the Balanced Scorecards for the entire college and for the administrative department.

- There is an alignment in the Balanced Scorecard between traditional performance measurement (the financial perspective) and the remaining metrics (the other three perspectives).

(b) A SAMPLE BALANCED SCORECARD FOR A SUPPORT AND SERVICE DEPARTMENT. In a liberal arts college there are likely to be a number of support and service departments, such as Campus Police, Buildings and Grounds, Maintenance, Janitorial, and Student Residence, to name some. Typically, support and service departments have no revenue, but do have costs. Like the academic departments and the administrative departments, support and service departments will also differ individually, but will also share many similar characteristics. Therefore, as in the case of an academic department or an administrative department, we can also visualize a support and service department. The support and service department is represented by the Balanced Scorecard in Exhibit 10a.8.

In Exhibit 10a.8 note the following important points:

- See how the metrics for the support and service department (in Exhibit 10a.8) differ from the metrics for the entire college (in Exhibit 10a.5).
- Also note the compatibility between the metrics for the support and service department (in Exhibit 10a.8) and the metrics for the entire college (in Exhibit 10a.5).
- On the one hand, there is necessarily a difference between the Balanced Scorecards for the entire college and for a support and service department. On the other hand, there is necessarily compatibility between the Balanced Scorecards for the entire college and for the support and service department.
- There is an alignment in the Balanced Scorecard between traditional performance measurement (the financial perspective) and the remaining metrics (the other three perspectives).

Certainly it requires considerable time, effort, and dedication for an organization to develop a sound and successful Balanced Scorecard project. "But wait," as they say, "there is more."

(c) MAINTAINING THE BALANCED SCORECARD SYSTEM. After the Balanced Scorecard system has been installed, it needs to be regularly maintained, and also adjustments will be required from time to time in order to cure any defects or shortcomings that may appear. In addition, there need to be regular checks that the metrics are valid early predictors of the lagging financial results. In some

Perspective	Objective	Metric	Target Value
Financial	Department total cost	Annual rate of growth	<5%
	Department head count	% Growth	<5%
	Department capital expenditures	Purchases of equipment	<$50,000
Customer	Maintain response time	Average time to respond	<1 day
	Improve client[a] satisfaction	Median score: client survey	>90%
	Quality of service	Demonstrate quality of service by competitive bid	Win all bids
Internal	Improve technology	% IT expense to revenue	>4%
	More powerful software	Ratio of new to old software products	>8%
	Avoid complaints	Ratio of complaints to compliments	<10%
Learning	Employee training	Annual hours of employee training	30
	Employee turnover	Employee turnover	<3%
	Employee pay	Average employee compensation	$32,000

[a] Clients of college administrative departments tend to be other organization units in the same college.

Exhibit 10a.8   Sample Metrics for a Support and Service Department

cases, this will be fairly straightforward. For example, in the Balanced Scorecard in Exhibit 10a.5, in the customer perspective, objectives include the number of students and the tuition per credit hour. Clearly any decline in those two metrics will result in a corresponding decline in the financial perspective, in the objectives of tuition revenue and operating surplus.

But in other cases, the connection between the early predictor metrics and the lagging financial objectives is not as clear. For instance, the links between the internal processes objective of technology improvement and financial results is not readily apparent. Nor is the link clear between the organizational learning objective of employee training and financial results. In these cases, it may be more practical simply to chart the actual metrics for each period and carefully eyeball them in order to watch out for how well one may track another, bearing in mind that there are likely to be lags and leads due to the presence of leading indicators in the nonfinancial metrics and lagging indicators in the financial metrics.

It is plain that successfully installing and maintaining a Balanced Scorecard system is a very demanding, very lengthy, and very intricate process. No organization should think otherwise. But despite the major effort required to adopt the Balanced Scorecard, it is equally clear that very many organizations have in fact adopted and retained the Balanced Scorecard system. So it is apparent that the benefits exceed the costs, and that the gain is worth the pain. The reason is that the benefits of successful strategy implementation and accurate performance evaluation of organizational units are extremely valuable, and are very difficult to obtain by any other means. It is important to appreciate how valuable it is to secure the following advantages that flow from successful use of the Balanced Scorecard:

- Enthusiastic involvement and participation by all staff members in their individual organizational units
- Coordination of all organizational units in executing the common strategy
- Creating the links between the daily routine tasks of each employee and the overall strategic goals of the entire organization

At the same time, it must be understood that no system is perfect. There are always areas for improvement, and there are always disadvantages as well as advantages to every system. The Balanced Scorecard is no exception.

(d) DRAWBACKS OF THE BALANCED SCORECARD SYSTEM. Despite its resounding success and very widespread adoption, the Balanced Scorecard has some disadvantages. Here are listed some drawbacks to consider:

- The Balanced Scorecard is very difficult to introduce successfully, and it is costly to maintain.
- The Balanced Scorecard relies on metrics, which are quantitative in nature. It may miss some qualitative aspects that are important. For example, in our example of a college master Balanced Scorecard, these problems might exist:
  - In the customer perspective, one objective states: "Increase student enrollment." But what if this is done by decreasing the quality of new students?
  - In the customer perspective, an objective states: "Improve satisfaction." But what if this is done by giving easier grades, so that no one ever gets less than an A, and employers become reluctant to hire these college graduates because it is impossible to know which ones are more competent or less competent?

Remember that what counts is what is counted. Therefore, numbers may tend to drive out softer measures of a qualitative nature that are more important, but that may seem less urgent. At the same time, we should not let the perfect be the enemy of the good. Despite a few possible blemishes, the Balanced Scorecard is a powerful and widely adopted system. Even though it is difficult and time-consuming to adopt and to maintain, its advantages plainly far outweigh its disadvantages, as its widespread popularity strongly suggests.

(e) IS THE BALANCED SCORECARD SUITED TO FOR-PROFIT COMPANIES OR NOT-FOR-PROFIT ORGANIZATIONS?   The Balanced Scorecard is very widely used, not only in business and industry but also in government agencies and not-for-profit organizations worldwide. The not-for-profit organizations range over many varied forms, including hospitals, universities, charities, foundations, and other kinds of enterprises. While the term Balanced Scorecard was first coined in the early 1990s, the roots of this type of approach stretch back to much earlier times. They include the pioneering work of General Electric on performance measurement reporting in the 1950s, as well as the creation of French process engineers (who conceived the *Tableau de Bord*—literally, a "dashboard" of performance measures) in the early part of the twentieth century.

The widespread use of the Balanced Scorecard in government agencies and not-for-profit organizations worldwide suggests that it is appropriate for use in both the for-profit sector as well as the not-for-profit and government agency sectors. That may well be the case. However, there may be an unanswered question that should perhaps be mentioned in this regard. A recent large survey found that financial performance is still by far the most measured feature of any business.[6] This survey reported that fully 87 percent of all respondents stated that they are measuring financial performance. The statistic that 16 percent of survey respondents were government agencies, as well as some other not-for-profit organizations, helps to explain why this is not 100 percent. If we exclude the government agencies and not-for-profit organizations, then the percentage of companies who measure financial performance becomes almost 100 percent. So the question is to what extent government agencies and perhaps also not-for-profit organizations do not measure financial performance. Economist Milton Friedman and his followers assert that government officials spend other people's money, rather than their own money.[7] They further assert that people take much less care when spending other people's money than they take when spending their own money.[8] If these assertions are true, then that is consistent with the survey finding that government agencies and perhaps also not-for-profit organizations do not measure financial performance. In that case, the Balanced Scorecard system may not work as well in government agencies and perhaps also in not-for-profit organizations as it works in business firms.

10a.5 EMPIRICAL STUDIES OF THE BALANCED SCORECARD SYSTEM

In 2012, in recognition of the 20th anniversary of the Balanced Scorecard, the Advanced Performance Institute (API) and Actuate surveyed more than 3,000 companies across all continents.[9] This is one of the largest and most comprehensive studies ever conducted in the field of enterprise performance management. The main participants were headquartered in North America (32 percent) and Europe (41 percent), followed by Australia (7 percent), Africa (6 percent), and South America (3 percent). These companies were asked about their use of performance measurement and the Balanced Scorecard.

The companies in the study varied from large multinational companies to small and medium-sized organizations. A valid cross section of size was achieved, with large organizations of 5,000 or more employees representing the largest individual group. The largest industry group is represented by the services sector, with almost a quarter of all participants falling into this category. It is trailed by government, retail and wholesale, manufacturing, and energy and utilities—each with around 10 percent.

---

[6] Balanced Scorecard 20yrsMeasuringManagingSurvey—a PDF file, available at www.ap-institute.com/media/468745/20yrsmeasuringmanagingsurvey-executivesummary.pdf.

[7] www.youtube.com/watch?v=k2Kg2SvsI8Q.

[8] A joke asks: Why are drunken sailors more ethical than politicians? Answer: Because the drunken sailors are wasting only their own money, unlike the politicians, who are wasting other people's money.

[9] Balanced Scorecard 20yrsMeasuringManagingSurvey—a PDF file, available at www.ap-institute.com/media/468745/20yrsmeasuringmanagingsurvey-executivesummary.pdf.

(a) WHICH BUSINESS PERSPECTIVES DO COMPANIES MEASURE AND MONITOR?   Data and performance indicators are vital to help us recognize whether enterprises are on the right track. While for most firms financial performance is the ultimate goal, financial information is only telling you whether you have done the right things in the past. Today's financial performance is a so-called lagging indicator that is not necessarily a valid predictor of future results. This is why companies are searching other areas of performance that may be leading indicators of future results, including how our customers are feeling about products and services, whether we are producing customer loyalty, whether we are improving internal efficiency, and whether we have involved the hearts and minds of our employees.

As mentioned, a recent survey found that financial performance is still by far the most measured feature of any business. Fully 87 percent of all respondents stated that they are measuring financial performance. The statistic that 16 percent of survey respondents were government agencies, as well as some other not-for-profit organizations, helps to explain why this is not 100 percent. If we exclude the government agencies and not-for-profit organizations, then the percentage of companies who measure financial performance becomes almost 100 percent.

The Balanced Scorecard is used by 38 percent of all companies in the study. The numbers are consistent with the results found by other research studies, and indicate that the use of this popular management tool is still on the rise. But even though satisfaction levels with the Balanced Scorecard seem to be high, previous studies have shown that many companies fail to apply the tool to its fullest potential. Therefore, there is still ample room for improvement.

Many performance management instruments have shown very high satisfaction ratings in previous user surveys. For example, a recent global survey of management tools conducted annually by Bain & Company shows that users of the Balanced Scorecard, mission and vision statements, and benchmarking report some of the highest satisfaction levels.

These results confirm what is often seen in practice, namely that performance management tools are seen as "something we do to aid senior management, so that they can assess performance levels." In order to be actually valued, everyone in the enterprise needs to secure benefits from performance measurement (and related management activities). It has to improve decision making at all levels of the organization. The study revealed that only 17 percent of respondents suppose that everyone in their company is receiving consistent insight from their performance measurement and management activities, improving day-to-day decision making.

The study identified significant factors that influence the level of approval with performance measurement and the level of benefits that establishments derive from their efforts to measure and manage performance. These factors help us establish the level of maturity of any approach. We find that the most mature implementations have the following factors in common:

- Buy-in and ownership of performance measurement is pervasive throughout the business.
- The reason for measuring and managing performance is internal and voluntary.
- Companies align strategic measures with operational measures.
- There is an alignment between traditional performance measurement and performance analytics.
- The focus of measuring and managing performance is both now and also the future.
- There is a focus on data quality.
- Companies use dedicated technology to measure and manage performance.

What many companies are struggling with is the alignment and integration between strategic and operational metrics. Operational measurement is too often still attempted without alignment with the strategic measures. This can cause a disconnect between strategic and operational objectives. What we find is that those organizations that are generating higher levels of benefits are those that integrate both a strategic and an operational approach to performance measurement. However, it is safe to conclude that the empirical studies just described are consistent with and fully able to confirm all statements made in this chapter.

10a.6 DISCUSSION QUESTIONS

- What is the Balanced Scorecard, and for what purposes is it used?
- Describe the main attributes of a Balanced Scorecard.
- Distinguish what a metric is, and give some examples of metrics, plus some examples of items that are not metrics. Explain why your examples are (or are a Balanced Scorecard as shown in Exhibit 10a.5).
- Create a Balanced Scorecard for any entity that you may wish. You may select a production department, an administrative department, or a support and service department. The choice is up to you. Whichever department you choose, be sure to include all four perspectives, each with three objectives, and a target metric for each objective.
- What are the limitations of the Balanced Scorecard?
- Create a Balanced Scorecard for the organizational unit in which you work, or used to work.

10a.7 RECOMMENDED REFERENCES ON THE BALANCED SCORECARD

The Balanced Scorecard Institute now has made available a selection of written training workbooks and the Balanced Scorecard Performance Toolkit. Other educational materials are available in video presentations.

(a) WRITTEN REFERENCE MATERIALS

The following written materials are recommended to provide help in special topics related to the balanced scorecard. Many of them may be found at Internet or retail outlets.

Bossidy, L., and R. Charan. *Execution: The Discipline of Getting Things Done*. New York: Crown, 2002. Best-seller by the CEO of AlliedSignal.

Brown, M. G., D. E. Hitchcock, and M. L. Willard. *Why TQM Fails and What to Do about It*. New York: McGraw-Hill, 1994. Lots of good advice that is still relevant.

Cartin, T. J. *Principles and Practices of TQM*. Milwaukee, WI: ASQC Quality Press, 1993. Practical guide to the concepts and tools of total quality management (TQM).

Cox, B. G., and B. N. Chinnappa. *Business Survey Methods*. New York: John Wiley & Sons, 1995. A good reference to help in the design of quality personal opinion and assessment surveys.

Deming, W. Edwards. *Out of the Crisis*. Cambridge, MA: MIT Center for Advanced Engineering Study, 1986. This is the classic book by Deming that summarized his teachings, which became the foundation for modern measurement-based management.

Drucker, P. *Innovation and Entrepreneurship*. New York: HarperBusiness, 1985. Ways that organizations can encourage new ideas, from the management guru who helped to inspire many of them.

Drucker, P. *Managing the Nonprofit Organization*. New York: HarperCollins, 1990. The wisdom of Drucker in his prime. If you are a nonprofit manager, you must get this book.

Fitz-enz, J., and J. Phillips. *A New Vision for Human Resources*. Seattle: Crisp Publications, 1998. Brief outline of measurement-based HR management by the well-respected founder of the Saratoga Institute.

Gabor, A. *The Man Who Discovered Quality*. New York: Penguin Books, 1990. An admirer's distillation of the teachings of—who else?—W. Edwards Deming.

Hodgetts, R. M. *Measures of Quality and High Performance*. New York: Amacom (American Management Association), 1998.

Juran, J. M. *Juran on Leadership for Quality*. New York: Free Press, 1989. Widely known author of the TQM era.

Kalton, G. *Introduction to Survey Sampling*. London: Sage Publications, 1983. A brief introduction to the mathematical analysis involved in surveys.

Kaplan, R. S., and D. P. Norton. *Alignment: Using the Balanced Scorecard to Create Corporate Synergies*. Boston: Harvard Business School Press, 2006. An advanced Balanced Scorecard book for large corporate enterprises.

Kaplan, R. S., and D. P. Norton. *The Balanced Scorecard: Translating Strategy into Action*. Boston: Harvard Business School Press, 1996. The book that coined the term, but does not include strategy maps because they weren't invented yet.

Kaplan, R. S., and D. P. Norton. *The Execution Premium*. Boston: Harvard Business School Press, 2008. Linking strategy to operations for competitive advantage.

Kaplan, R. S., and D. P. Norton. *The Strategy-Focused Organization: How Balanced Scorecard Companies Thrive in the New Business Environment*. Boston: Harvard Business School Press, 2001. Recommended for a manager's introduction to the key concepts.

Kaplan, R. S., and D. P. Norton. *Strategy Maps: Converting Intangible Assets into Tangible Outcomes*. Boston: Harvard Business School Press, 2004. Offers 400 pages of private-sector strategy maps; 28 pages of government and not-for-profit strategy maps.

Kaydos, W. *Measuring, Managing, and Maximizing Performance: What Every Manager Needs to Know about Quality and Productivity to Make Real Improvements in Performance*. New York: Productivity Press, 1991. The title says it all.

Kaydos, W. *Operational Performance Measurement: Increasing Total Productivity*. Boca Raton, FL: CRC Press, 1998. An excellent treatment by one of our own consultants.

Keehley, P., et al. *Benchmarking for Best Practices in the Public Sector: Achieving Performance Breakthroughs in Federal, State and Local Agencies*. San Francisco: Jossey-Bass, 1997. Explains the processes used in conducting benchmarking projects between governmental organizations.

Leidig, G., and T. Mayer (Hrsg.). *Betriebswirtschaft und Mediengesellschaft im Wandel. Festschrift für Diethelm Schmidt und Lorenz Rottland*. Wiesbaden: Bundesverband Druck und Medien (German Printing Association), 2002 (xviii + 365 pp., ISBN 3-88701-237-2).

Leidig, G., and R. Sommerfeld. *Balanced Scorecard als Instrument zur Strategieumsetzung. Handbuch für die Druck- und Medienindustrie*. Wiesbaden: Bundesverband Druck und Medien (German Printing Association), 2002 (391 pp. incl. CD-ROM, ISBN 3-88701-238-0).

McCormack, C., and D. Jones. *Building a Web-Based Education System*. New York: Wiley Computer Publishing, 1997. Includes software to support all aspects of training.

Miller, G. J., W. B. Hildreth, and J. Rabin. *Performance Based Budgeting: An ASPA Classic*. Boulder, CO: Westview Press, 2001. An anthology of the best academic articles on this subject. Includes an important article by ex-Senator Fred Thompson.

Mintzberg, H., B. Ahlstrand, and J. Lampel. *Strategy Safari: A Guided Tour Through the Wilds of Strategic Management*. New York: Free Press, 1998. Classic but advanced book that describes 10 schools of strategic management.

Monahan, K. E. *Balanced Measures for Strategic Planning: A Public Sector Handbook*. Vienna, VA: Management Concepts, 2001. Outgrowth of a study done for the National Partnership for Reinventing Government (NPRG). A practical reference book with numerous public-sector case studies.

Olson, A., et al. *Performance Measurement*. Arlington, VA: Coopers & Lybrand, 1995. A monograph by a leading supplier of management consulting to the U.S. federal government.

Olve, N., J. Roy, and M. Wetter. *Making Scorecards Actionable: Balancing Strategy and Control*, English ed. Hoboken, NJ: John Wiley & Sons, 2003. An update on progress with the Balanced Scorecard in several mostly Scandinavian companies.

Olve, N., J. Roy, and M. Wetter. *Performance Drivers: A Practical Guide to Using the Balanced Scorecard*, English ed. New York: John Wiley & Sons, 1999. The Swedish approach to the Balanced Scorecard.

Pederson, L. M. *Performance-Oriented Management: A Practical Guide for Government Agencies*. Vienna, VA: Management Concepts, 2002. Includes how to facilitate offsite strategic planning retreats, develop performance management systems, and conduct Baldrige assessments. Contains several assessment tools in appendixes.

Raj, D. *Sampling Theory*. New York: McGraw-Hill, 1968. Textbook on survey and experimental design.

Savage, S. L. *Decision Making with Insight*. Belmont, CA: Brooks/Cole—Thomson Learning, 2003. Contains software for making analytical decision models and Monte Carlo simulations with Excel spreadsheets.

Shewhart, W. "Statistical Method from the Viewpoint of Quality Control." In Deming, W. E., ed., Washington, DC: Graduate School of the Department of Agriculture, 1939. Shewhart was the inventor of Statistical Process Control (SPC), which was an early form of performance measurement and control of industrial processes.

Tingey, M. O. *Comparing ISO 9000, Malcolm Baldrige and the SEI CMM for Software.* Upper Saddle River, NJ: Prentice-Hall, 1997. A reference and selection guide for these three quality management assessment methodologies.

Van Grembergen, W. *Information Technology Evaluation Methods & Management.* London: Idea Group Publishing, 2001. Collection of scholarly studies by various authors that includes Balanced Scorecard concepts as they relate to IT management.

Wholey, J. S., H. P. Hatry, and K. E. Newcomer, eds. *Handbook of Practical Program Evaluation.* San Francisco: Jossey-Bass, 1994. A major 600-page textbook written by key leaders in U.S. government program evaluation.

An extensive list of additional books and articles is available at the website of the Performance Measurement Association (www.performanceportal.org).

(b) RECOMMENDED BALANCED SCORECARD VIDEOS

The Balanced Scorecard

www.youtube.com/watch?v=oNy8kupW8oI

Nov. 2, 2011—Uploaded by HBSExecEd

Balanced Scorecard by Steve Wallace, 14,726 views; 8:24. Watch Later Balanced Score Card, Video #1, Part. . .

Balanced Score Card, Video #1, Part A

www.youtube.com/watch?v=FDpVT6-waDM

Aug. 10, 2009—Uploaded by Nevin Mann

Balanced Scorecard approach to strategic planning. A new process that assures effective efficient. . .

Balanced Scorecard

www.youtube.com/watch?v=M_IlOlywryw

Aug. 9, 2012—Uploaded by IntrafocusUK

A visual summary of what the Balanced Scorecard is and how it relates to business. . . You need Adobe Flash. . .

Balanced Scorecard Approach

www.youtube.com/watch?v=ZOJNgs-_83g

Jun. 21, 2011—Uploaded by B2Bwhiteboard

This video covers the development of the balanced scorecard approach to measuring corporate performance. . .

Strategic Planning with the Balanced Scorecard

www.youtube.com/watch?v=AdXt8BfiGJg

Dec. 17, 2009—Uploaded by virtualstrategist

Alert icon. You need Adobe Flash Player to watch this video. . . Balanced Score Card, Video #1, Part A by. . .

Perform Mgt & Eval.—2Balanced Scorecard

www.youtube.com/watch?v=iI8ZmLwqElI

Oct. 1, 2007—Uploaded by Susan Crosson

Managerial Accounting SFCC Fall 2007 Chapter 8 Videos. . . Thumbnail Balanced Scorecard Implementation. . .

Balanced Scorecard at a Hospital Video

www.youtube.com/watch?v=V39QPvX-ksg

Jan. 6, 2012—Uploaded by BalancedScorecardz

This Balanced Scorecard was built for a regional hospital to aid in its integration of two other health sytems. . .

USDC—The Balanced Scorecard on Vimeo

vimeo.com/31819871

Nov. 9, 2011

. . . introduction to the Balanced Scorecard, its implementation at UCSD, . . . that you appreciate, enjoy. . .

The Balanced Scorecard

www.youtube.com/watch?v=3xsE4EvzQAg

Oct. 23, 2008—Uploaded by fkaiser007

Summary of the Balanced Scorecard, a management approach to align various business. . . You need Adobe. . .

Balanced Scorecard

www.youtube.com/watch?v=OvvsFro636w

May 24, 2012—Uploaded by dadufv

Webinar: Balanced Scorecard—11/30/2011 by Litebi, 259 views; 5:18. Watch Later BSC Teil 1 by KapplerAr 9. . .

CHAPTER 12

REVENUES AND RECEIVABLES (REVISED)

Alan S. Glazer, PhD, CPA
Franklin & Marshall College

Cynthia L. Krom, PhD, CPA, CFE
Franklin & Marshall College

Henry R. Jaenicke, PhD, CPA
Late of Drexel University

12.4 TYPES OF REVENUE TRANSACTIONS

Replaces text on pages 12 · 43 through 12 · 44 in main edition

(d) FINANCIAL ACCOUNTING STANDARDS BOARD PROJECT ON REVENUE RECOGNITION. In mid-2002, the Financial Accounting Standards Board (FASB) formally recognized the need to provide additional guidance and to promote international convergence of accounting standards for revenue recognition. It initiated a joint project with the International Accounting Standards Board (IASB) to eliminate inconsistencies in the authoritative literature and to provide a conceptual foundation for resolving new and emerging revenue recognition and measurement issues. The project's two components were (1) the reorganization of U.S. generally accepted accounting principles (GAAP) into a more user-friendly single source of authoritative standards and (2) the clarification of the principles for recognizing revenue with the goal of developing a common revenue standard for U.S. GAAP and International Financial Reporting Standards.

In June 2010, the FASB published an Exposure Draft for public comment of proposed Accounting Standards Update (ASU) No. 1820-100, *Revenue Recognition (Topic 605): Revenue from Contracts with Customers*. The IASB Exposure Draft was similar except for minor differences in spelling, style, and format. After reviewing almost 1,000 comment letters, the boards agreed that some redrafting was necessary.

In November 2011, the boards issued a 217-page revised Exposure Draft to provide additional guidance supporting the new requirements' core principle: "an entity shall recognize revenue to depict the transfer of promised goods or services to customers in an amount that reflects the consideration to which the entity expects to be entitled in exchange for those goods or services" (par. 3). The FASB expects to issue a new Accounting Standards Update, and the IASB expects to issue a new IFRS in the second half of 2013. The new requirements for U.S. GAAP would be applicable for annual and interim reporting periods beginning on or after January 1, 2017[1]; the IFRS requirements would be effective on January 1, 2017. As a result, public companies with calendar year-ends would be required to apply the new requirements in their first quarters ending March 31, 2017; early application of the FASB requirements would not be permitted.

As of this writing, the proposed new standard would replace much of the current guidance on revenue recognition for customer contracts with a five-step approach[2]:

1. Identify contracts with customers. Contracts can be written, verbal, or implied and must have "commercial substance" and be approved by all parties who are committed to meet their obligations under the contract. In addition, the entity must be able to identify all rights regarding the goods or services to be transferred and the payment terms (p. 3).

2. Identify separate performance obligations in customer contracts. A good or service would be considered a separate obligation if it is both "distinct" (i.e., the customer can benefit from the good or service on its own or with other easily available resources) and distinct in the contract's context (i.e., the performance objective is not highly dependent on, or interrelated with, other promised goods or services).

3. Determine transaction prices (i.e., the consideration the entity expects to receive in exchange for the promised goods or services). This includes the effects of variable and noncash consideration, the time value of money, and consideration payable to customers. Adjustments for collectability (i.e., expected bad debts) would be reported as operating expenses and, if material, shown as a separate line item.

4. Allocate transaction prices to separate performance obligations based on relative stand-alone selling prices. When those prices cannot be directly observed, various estimation approaches would be used, relying to the extent possible on observable inputs (e.g., market prices for similar goods or services).

5. Recognize revenue when each separate performance obligation is satisfied (i.e., when control over the goods or services is transferred to customers). Revenue would be recognized over time if certain criteria are met, and progress toward completion would be measured using input or output methods. Otherwise, revenue would be recognized at the point where control is transferred to customers.

The new standard also is expected to increase qualitative and quantitative revenue-related disclosures. For example, public entities would be required to disclose:

- Management judgments, and changes in those judgments, used in determining the timing and amount of revenue recognized during the period
- Types of goods and services provided to customers, significant payment terms, and other information related to performance obligations
- Disaggregated revenue information reconciled to total reported revenues and how that information relates to entities' segment disclosures
- Beginning and ending balances in contract assets, contract liabilities, and receivables from customer contracts and significant changes in those accounts

---

[1] FASB. "Project Updates—Revenue Recognition—Joint Project of the FASB and IASB." June 4, 2013. "Effective Date" section.

[2] FASB Revised Exposure Draft of Proposed Accounting Standards Update. *Revenue Recognition (Topic 605): Revenue from Contracts with Customers (Including Proposed Amendments to the* FASB Accounting Standards Codification). January 4, 2012, and November 14, 2011, p. 2.

- Methods and assumptions used to estimate transaction prices and to allocate amounts to performance obligations
- Aggregate amounts of transaction prices allocated to incomplete performance obligations and when future revenues from those obligations are expected to be recognized
- Capitalized costs of obtaining or fulfilling contracts and information about accounting policies related to those costs
- Certain information in interim periods

Transition to the new standard would be disclosed using a modified retrospective approach. That is, in the period of initial application, entities would record a cumulative catch-up adjustment only for existing contracts still requiring performance by the entity. Although restatement of prior period results would not be required, entities would have to disclose pro forma results assuming that their old methods of revenue recognition were used. Those disclosures would allow statement users to compare reported results with those that would have been reported using the entities' old revenue recognition methods.

12.8 SOURCES AND SUGGESTED REFERENCES

New entry

Financial Accounting Standards Board. Revised Exposure Draft of Proposed Accounting Standards Update. *Revenue Recognition (Topic 605): Revenue from Contracts with Customers (Including Proposed Amendments to the* FASB Accounting Standards Codification). Norwalk, CT: Author, November 2011 and January 2012.

ASSIGNING INDIRECT MANUFACTURING COSTS TO PRODUCTS (NEW)

Les Livingstone, MBA, PhD, CPA (NY & TX)
University of Maryland, University College

Some manufacturing costs can be directly traced to products, and are known as direct costs. Other costs cannot be directly traced to products, and are known as indirect costs. For example, consider a company that makes golf clubs and tennis rackets by assembling components purchased from suppliers. First, we focus on direct product costs.

13a.1 DIRECT PRODUCT COSTS

Golf clubs and tennis rackets are made from the following components:

Golf Clubs	Tennis Rackets
Club heads	Racket frames
Club shafts	Racket strings
Club grips	Racket grips

For golf clubs the costs of the club heads, club shafts, and club grips can be traced from outside supplier invoices, and accounted for as raw material costs. For tennis rackets the costs of the racket frames, racket strings, and racket grips can also be traced from outside supplier invoices, and accounted for as raw material costs. So, direct raw material costs can be traced to the respective product lines of golf clubs and tennis rackets.

Similarly, the direct labor costs of assembling golf clubs and tennis rackets can be traced to the product lines of golf clubs and tennis rackets. The time cards of factory workers can identify how many hours each worker spent on each product line.

We conclude that both raw materials and factory labor can usually be regarded as direct product costs because their amounts can generally be traced straight to individual products. But there are other product costs that also must be considered. These product costs cannot be traced straight to individual products.

13a.2 INDIRECT PRODUCT COSTS

Imagine that the assembly of golf clubs and tennis rackets takes place in a rented facility. The costs of this facility are rent, insurance, security, cleaning, water, electric power, telephone, postage and delivery, and depreciation of machinery and equipment. These combined costs are often known as manufacturing overhead.[1] Most of these costs are fixed, meaning that they do not increase or decrease according to the level of manufacturing activity. Of course, fixed costs do not vary with the level of manufacturing activity. But they may vary due to other factors. For example, factory rent or delivery expenses may change simply because a supplier has increased the price charged, or because a cheaper source has been found for purchasing security or cleaning services. So the term *fixed* refers only to costs that do not increase or decrease **according to the level of manufacturing activity**. But these fixed costs may vary for factors other than the level of manufacturing activity.

It is very difficult (if not impossible) to trace these manufacturing overhead costs to the product lines of golf clubs and tennis rackets. For example, it is hard to know how much of the telephone expense relates to golf clubs and how much to tennis rackets. It is even harder to distinguish the telephone expense for golf clubs with steel shafts versus graphite shafts, or tennis rackets with gut strings versus nylon strings. So direct product costs like raw materials and factory labor can readily be traced to product lines, but indirect product costs cannot be traced to product lines. Therefore, indirect product costs must be allocated—or assigned—to product lines. The term *allocated* means assigned to product lines either by some formula or by arbitrary means.

Traditional cost systems allocate manufacturing overhead costs to individual product lines in an arbitrary manner, usually by means of a single allocation base, such as direct labor hours. For example, imagine that manufacturing overhead costs total $800,000 for the month of May. Direct labor hours in May total 6,450, of which 2,560 hours are for tennis rackets and 3,890 hours are for golf clubs. Then manufacturing overhead costs are allocated as shown in Exhibit 13a.1.

It is typically unknown whether this allocation is accurate. In fact, it can be accurate only if manufacturing overhead costs are actually driven by direct labor hours. This seems unlikely in most cases, because direct labor hours often vary according to the level of manufacturing activity. But manufacturing overhead costs tend to include fixed costs as well as variable costs. So manufacturing overhead costs do not vary according to the level of manufacturing activity, because they include fixed costs. Therefore traditional cost allocations are frequently inaccurate and unreliable. As a result, product decisions by management can likewise be inaccurate and unreliable.

Item	Tennis	Golf	Total
Direct labor hours	2,560	3,890	6,450
Direct labor hours %	39.7%	60.3%	100.0%
Manufacturing overhead allocation[1]	39.7% of $800,000 = $317,600	60.3% of $800,000 = $482,400	$800,000
Number of units produced	12,000 rackets	20,000 clubs	
Manufacturing overhead allocation per unit	$26.47	$24.12	

Exhibit 13a.1   Allocation of Manufacturing Overhead to Tennis Rackets and Golf Clubs

[1] Note that manufacturing overhead does not include selling, general, and administrative expenses, and does not include interest expense or income tax expense. Only manufacturing costs are assigned or allocated to products.

This is a serious problem, because incorrect product cost estimates frequently lead to incorrect product pricing decisions. In turn, incorrect product pricing decisions often lead to competitive disadvantages, and possibly even to bankruptcy.

13a.3 ACTIVITY-BASED COSTING

In order to provide more accurate and reliable allocations of manufacturing overhead costs, activity-based costing was developed. Instead of a single allocation base, activity-based costing uses separate cost pools and allocation bases for different activities. Each cost pool is allocated to individual product lines based on whatever driver causes the costs in each pool to be incurred by each individual product line.

For example, one cost pool may consist of all costs relating to machinery and equipment, such as maintenance and depreciation of machinery and equipment, plus a share of the rent, insurance, and electric power costs. Assume that all machinery and equipment are used to assemble golf clubs, and that tennis rackets are gripped and strung completely by hand. Then clearly, all machinery and equipment costs will be allocated to golf clubs, and none to tennis rackets. This is a more accurate allocation than traditional costing (based on a single allocator, such as direct labor hours) can provide. Under traditional costing, using direct labor hours to allocate manufacturing overhead costs to product lines, machinery and equipment costs would be allocated partly to golf clubs, and partly to tennis rackets—which would be incorrect.

Activity-based costing is more accurate and reliable than traditional costing because:

- It uses multiple cost pools, which traditional costing (based on a single allocator, such as direct labor hours) cannot provide.
- It is based on a number of different activities.
- It is used to allocate costs to product lines and employs appropriate cost drivers.

Costs of direct materials and direct labor are not difficult to trace to different product lines. But indirect manufacturing overhead costs are very difficult to trace to different product lines. Traditional cost systems use arbitrary single allocators (like direct labor hours) to assign indirect manufacturing overhead costs to different product lines. The resulting allocations are often inaccurate and unreliable. This leads to serious problems, and may even imperil the entire enterprise.

Activity-based costing is more accurate and reliable than traditional costing in allocating indirect manufacturing overhead costs to different product lines. Therefore, the greater the proportion of indirect manufacturing overhead costs to direct material and labor costs, the greater is the need for activity-based costing. And, since indirect manufacturing overhead costs tend to be fixed costs, the greater the proportion of fixed costs to variable costs and the greater the advantage of activity-based costing over traditional costing.

At the same time, there are also drawbacks to the introduction of activity-based costing. One such drawback is the cost of installing and maintaining an accurate system of activity-based costing. Another factor to consider is the cost versus the benefit of activity-based costing.

For example, a cost accounting system can (in theory) track the cost of every paper clip, every lead pencil, and every eraser. But we often settle for a simpler (and less expensive) system of calculating product cost. Since the cost of scraps of cloth is quite low, we probably tend to treat this total cost as an item of indirect cost, instead of tracing it directly to every auto repair completed. In brief, simpler treatment tends to be less expensive than more elaborate treatment, and therefore cost accounting tends to follow a cost-benefit calculation, whereby smaller and less complex organizations tend to use less complex systems that only larger and more complex organizations can afford.

In order to further illustrate the use of product cost allocation, we present the following cases based on actual experience. The first case to be presented is the Grace Design case, which requires an understanding of breakeven analysis.

Breakeven analysis, as the name implies, is a method of finding the volume of production where there is neither a profit nor a loss, but rather a breakeven point. This handbook explains breakeven analysis in Chapter 29 (Cost-Volume-Revenue Analysis for Nonprofit Organizations), and the following material that makes use of breakeven analysis is based on principles from Chapter 29. Therefore, if you are not familiar with breakeven analysis, it would be most desirable to read Chapter 29 before proceeding further with this present chapter and reading the Grace Design case.

13a.4 THE GRACE DESIGN CASE

Jane Goodheart established and runs a small workshop that manufactures costume jewelry repro-ductions of well-known jewelry masterpieces by Faberge and other famous designers, plus antique pieces of Etruscan, Russian, Egyptian, Chinese, and French jewelry. She markets these creations to museums across the United States in batches of 12 assorted items, for which she charges $680 per batch. In turn, the museums sell the jewelry at prices averaging nine times what they paid for the jewelry.

Jane's only assistant is Joe, who is paid $15 per hour for his unskilled labor. Jewelry production varies between a low of four batches and a high of six batches per week, and averages 200 batches per year. Each batch costs $80 (excluding wages) to pack and ship, with Joe doing all the packing and shipping. It takes Joe two hours to pack and ship one batch. Joe also does other chores, such as sweeping, vacuuming, and cleaning, and he averages 20 hours per week of employment with Jane's workshop, for the 40 weeks per year that he works for Jane.

Jane spends 10 weeks a year touring the United States and attending trade shows in order to sell her jewelry and to find suppliers of semiprecious stones, beads, and other components for her products. Her travel, hotel, and food costs are $6,050 each year. Workshop rent and utilities cost her an average of $300 per week. Jane works 40 weeks a year at making jewelry, and sublets the workshop for its cost in rent and utilities during her 10-week tour plus her two weeks of vacation each year.

The cost of rent, utilities, and raw materials varies from $2,300 per week when four batches are produced to $2,800 per week in weeks when five batches are produced, and to $3,300 per week when six batches per week are manufactured. Business has been brisk, and Jane could easily sell every batch that she produces. But she finds herself earning very little profit, and after paying her 28 percent income tax, she has almost no money to live on. That is what has led Jane to you, as her consultant. She complains to you that she works very hard, 50 weeks a year, but ends up broke and frustrated. Jane says that her tastes are modest and emphasize artistry rather than material possessions. She notes that she would be quite satisfied to make $25,000 a year, after taxes.

You agree to analyze her business operations and to advise her how to reach her modest goal of earning $25,000 per year, after taxes. After some calculation and some thought, you conclude that Jane has to increase her revenues, probably by raising her selling price. See Exhibit 13a.2 and Exhibit 13a.3.

The Grace Design case uses breakeven analysis to determine a desired after-tax annual income for the owner. As noted in Chapter 29, breakeven analysis is a widely used technique often applied to solve problems. Like most techniques, though, breakeven analysis has limitations. For one thing, it is a single-period model that deals with just one point in time, and does not look beyond that single period—making it static rather than dynamic (multiperiod) in nature. Further, breakeven analysis applies only to single-product organizations, rather than to multiproduct establishments. It can be adapted in a limited manner to multiproduct organizations, but only those that maintain a fixed mix of products in a constant ratio.

However, breakeven analysis can be most helpful in solving a number of different problems. For instance, as described in Chapter 29, breakeven analysis can not only find the point at which volume switches from loss to profit (as the name "breakeven analysis" implies). But it can also be used to predetermine any given level of profit, as we illustrated in the Grace Design case. Further, breakeven analysis is useful in confronting uncertainty by means of calculating a "best case" and a "worst case" result. The calculation of a best case and a worst case may use a high volume and a low volume of business, where the actual volume of business is very uncertain. Or perhaps the level of

Revenue	Quantity	Current Income Statement	Proposed Income Statement
Average # of batches per week sold	5		5
× Weeks per year	40		40
× Price per batch	$ 680		$ 904
Revenue		$ 136,000	$ 180,772
Variable Costs			
Variable cost per batch*	500		
× Average # of batches per week sold	5		
× Weeks per year	40	$ 100,000	$ 100,000
Packaging and shipping per batch	80		
× Average # batches per week sold	5		
× Weeks per year	40	$ 16,000	$ 16,000
Joe's hours per batch for processing	2		
× Joe's wage per hour	15		
× Average # batches per week sold	5		
× Weeks per year	40	$ 6,000	$ 6,000
Batches per year	200		
Total variable costs		$ 122,000	$ 122,000
Variable cost per batch		$ 610	$ 610
Fixed Costs			
Other fixed costs per year**		$ 12,000	$ 12,000
Joe's hours per batch for processing	2		
× Average # batches per week sold	5		
× Weeks per year	40		
Joe's hours per year for processing	400		
Joe's total hours per year: 20 hours × 40 weeks	800		
Joe's hours per year on other chores	400		
× Joe's wage per hour	15	$ 6,000	$ 6,000
Fixed costs for 10-week jewelry show visits		$ 6,050	$ 6,050
Total fixed costs		$ 24,050	$ 24,050
Total costs		$ 146,050	$ 146,050
Contribution			
Total revenue less variable costs		$ 14,000	$ 58,772
Profit/Loss			
Total revenue less total costs for 200 batches a year		−$ 10,050	**$ 34,722**
Jane is losing money by producing below her breakeven point, annually			−$ 10,050
Breakeven			
Selling price per batch		$ 680	$ 904
Less: Variable cost per batch		$ 610	$ 610
Contribution per batch		$ 70	$ 294
Total fixed costs		24,050	$ 24,050
Breakeven — in batches		344	**344**
Breakeven batches with desired income of $25,000		701	**701**

Exhibit 13a.2   Grace Design: Analysis of Profitability and Goals

Proposal

After-tax profit desired		$ 25,000	
Adjust to pretax basis		$ 34,722	
Adjusted revenue required		$ 180,772	
Divide by 200 batches		$ 904	
Raise selling price to		$ 904	per batch
Jane's income before tax		$ 34,722	
Less tax	28.00%	$ 9,722	
Jane's income after tax		$ 25,000	
Which matches her desired annual income of		$ 25,000	

Solution

Increase price per batch from	$ 680	to	$ 904

This price increase is feasible because the case states that:

    a. Business was brisk, and Jane could easily sell every batch that she produced.

    b. The museums sold the jewelry at prices averaging nine times what they paid for the jewelry.

With the increased price Jane will earn her desired annual income of	$ 25,000

Other Costs

Batches produced per week	4	5	6
Other costs per week	$ 2,300	$ 2,800	$ 3,300
Extra cost per batch		$ 500	$ 500
*Therefore variable cost per batch is		$ 500	
And other fixed cost per week is		$ 300	for workshop rent and utilities
× Weeks per year		40	
**Other fixed costs per year are		$ 12,000	

Cost Function

Since for each batch, variable costs
are $500, then fixed cost per week is $300
So the cost function for other costs = $300
(fixed cost) + $500 X(batch variable cost)
where X = # of batches

Exhibit 13a.3   Grace Design: Solution

uncertainty relates to the price to be charged for a product, which might be very difficult to predict—especially for a new product, which has no past history. Yet another source of future uncertainty is whether the level of foreign exchange rates is likely to increase or decrease. In fact, many business decisions involve significant future uncertainty, so breakeven analysis is often used and useful.

13a.5 THE PHILBY MANUFACTURING CASE

Next, we explore setting a price on a custom product, compared to a standard product. In order to do so, we use the Philby Manufacturing case as a vehicle to promote further understanding of cost tracing and cost assignment by means of cost allocation techniques.

    Philby Manufacturing Company produces two cello models. One is a standard acoustic cello that sells for $600 and is constructed from medium-grade material. The other model is a custom-made amplified cello with pearl inlays and a body constructed from special woods. The custom cello sells for $900. Both cellos require 10 hours of direct labor to produce, but the custom cello is manufactured by more experienced workers who are paid at a higher rate.

Cello	Standard	Custom
Volume in unit	900	100
Unit selling price	$ 600.00	$ 900.00
Unit Costs		
Direct materials	$ 150.00	$ 375.00
Direct labor	$ 180.00	$ 240.00
Manufacturing overhead*	$ 135.00	$ 135.00
Total unit costs	$ 465.00	$ 750.00
Unit gross profit	$ 135.00	$ 150.00
Direct labor hours	10.00	10.00
Direct labor rate per hour	$ 18.00	$ 24.00
Manufacturing Overhead Costs		
Building depreciation	$ 40,000	
Maintenance	$ 15,000.00	
Purchasing	$ 20,000.00	
Inspection	$ 12,000.00	
Indirect materials	$ 15,000.00	
Supervision	$ 30,000.00	
Supplies	$ 3,000.00	
Total manufacturing overhead	$ 135,000.00	

Exhibit 13a.4   Philby Manufacturing Case

Most of Philby's sales come from the standard cello, but sales of the custom model have been growing. Exhibit 13a.4 presents the company's sales, production, and cost information for last year.

The manufacturing overhead costs are fixed in nature: They do not vary with the volume of manufacturing. The company allocates overhead costs using the traditional method. Its activity base is direct labor hours. The predetermined overhead rate, based on 10,000 direct labor hours, is $13.50 per direct labor hour ($135,000 ÷ 10,000 direct labor hours). Johann Brahms, president of Philby, is concerned that the cost-allocation system the company is using may not be generating accurate information and that the selling price of the custom cello may not be covering its true cost.

The cost-allocation system Philby has been using allocates 90 percent of overhead costs to the standard cello because 90 percent of direct labor hours are spent on the standard model. (See Exhibit 13a.5.)

13a.6 LESSONS LEARNED

Traditional manufacturing overhead allocation by just a single allocator can be very inaccurate. Activity-based costing can be much more accurate. Activity-based costing requires more information than traditional cost allocation, and is therefore a more expensive system. Since traditional cost allocation can lead to poor product decisions, activity-based costing can be well worth its extra cost. Products sold at a loss should not necessarily be discontinued.

As long as a product sells for more than its variable cost, it is contributing to profit, and should be continued.

This is true even if the product is below its unit breakeven volume.

Question: What overhead was allocated to each of the two models last year?

	Total	# of Cellos	Per Cello
Total overhead	$ 135,000	1,000	$ 135.00
Standard cello: 90%	$ 121,500	900	$ 135.00
Custom cello: 10%	$ 13,500	100	$ 135.00

Question: Why might this not be an accurate way to assign overhead costs to products?
Response: Both cellos require 10 hours of direct labor to produce, but the custom cello is manufactured by more experienced and higher-paid workers.
Question: How would the use of more than one cost pool improve Philby's costing?
Response: At present all indirect manufacturing costs are allocated on direct labor hours. But direct labor hours may not be the basis upon which indirect manufacturing costs are incurred for the standard and the custom cellos — just as direct labor hours do not allow for the higher pay of the workers making custom cellos.
Philby's controller developed the following data for use in activity-based costing:

Manufacturing Overhead Cost	Amount	Cost Driver	Standard Cello	Custom Cello
Building depreciation	$ 40,000	Square footage	3,000	1,000
Maintenance	$ 15,000	Direct labor hours	9,000	1,000
Purchasing	$ 20,000	# of purchase orders	1,500	500
Inspection	$ 12,000	# of inspections	400	600
Indirect materials	$ 15,000	# of units made	900	100
Supervision	$ 30,000	# of inspections	400	600
Supplies	$ 3,000	# of units made	900	100
Total	$ 135,000			

Task: Use activity based costing to allocate the costs of overhead per unit and in total to each model of cello.

Allocation Basis

Manufacturing Overhead Cost	Amount	Cost Driver	Standard Cello	Custom Cello
Building depreciation	$ 40,000	Square footage	3,000	1,000
Maintenance	$ 15,000	Direct labor hours	9,000	1,000
Purchasing	$ 20,000	# of purchase orders	1,500	500
Inspection	$ 12,000	# of inspections	400	600
Indirect materials	$ 15,000	# of units	900	100
Supervision	$ 30,000	# of inspections	400	600
Supplies	$ 3,000	# of units	900	100
Total overhead cost	$ 135,000	(Fixed regardless of how many cellos made)		

Overhead Cost per Cello (Divide by Unit Volume)
Overhead Cost

Manufacturing Overhead Cost	Amount	Standard Cello	Custom Cello
Building depreciation	$ 40,000	$ 30,000	$ 10,000
Maintenance	$ 15,000	$ 13,500	$ 1,500
Purchasing	$ 20,000	$ 15,000	$ 5,000
Inspection	$ 12,000	$ 4,800	$ 7,200
Indirect materials	$ 15,000	$ 13,500	$ 1,500
Supervision	$ 30,000	$ 12,000	$ 18,000
Supplies	$ 3,000	$ 2,700	$ 300
Total overhead cost	$ 135,000	$ 91,500	$ 43,500
Overhead cost per cello		$ 101.67	$ 435.00

Exhibit 13a.5   Philby Manufacturing Case—Solution

Task: Calculate the cost of a custom cello using activity-based costing.

Direct materials	$ 375.00
Direct labor	$ 240.00
Allocated overhead cost	$ 0.00
Total manufacturing cost	$ 615.00

Question: Why is the cost different from the cost calculated using the traditional allocation method?

Per Unit	Standard Cello	Custom Cello	
Direct materials	$ 150.00	$ 375.00	Traced
Direct labor	$ 180.00	$ 240.00	Traced
Allocated overhead cost	$ 101.67	$ 435.00	Allocated
Total manufacturing cost	$ 431.67	$ 1,050.00	
Selling price	$ 600.00	$ 900.00	
Gross profit	$ 168.33	−$ 150.00	
Gross profit % of selling price	28.06%	−16.67%	

Raw material and direct labor can be traced, but overhead is allocated by activity-based costing.
Question: At the current selling price, is the company covering its true cost of production?
Response: For the standard cello, the selling price of $600 is greater than the unit manufacturing cost of $431.67 and yields a reasonable gross profit on selling price. But for the custom cello, the selling price of $900 does not cover the manufacturing cost, and yields a gross loss on each custom cello.
Question: What course of action might Philby Manufacturing follow?
Response: Philby Manufacturing should increase the price of the custom cello to earn at least the same % gross profit as on the standard cello.
It makes sense that Philby Manufacturing should have as much pricing flexibility on the custom cello as on the standard cello.
For example, let the selling price of the custom cello be X.

30% gross profit on selling price is:
30% = X less cost/price divided by X
$30.00\% = (X − \$1,050/X)/X$
$70.00\% \times (X − \$1,050/X)/X = \$1,050.00$
So $X = \$1,500.00$
Check the answer:
This results in:

Unit selling price	$ 1,500.00
Unit manufacturing cost	$ 1,050.00
Unit gross profit	$ 450.00
Gross profit % to sales	30.00%

The answer checks out as correct.

So Philby Manufacturing should increase the selling price of the custom cello to $1,500.
We assume that 100 custom cellos can still be sold each year at the price of $1,500 each.
Question: What should Philby Manufacturing do if the quantity of custom cellos sold at the new price falls to 50 per year?
If the custom cello at a price of $1,500 sells only 50 units per year, then the unit contribution is:

	Unit Volume	Per Unit	Total
Revenue	50	$ 1,500	$ 75,000
Variable cost: Direct material	50	$ 375	$ 18,750
Direct labor	50	$ 240	$ 12,000
Contribution	50	$ 885	$ 44,250

Exhibit 13a.5   (Continued)

Since it is still profitable at 50 units per year, Philby Manufacturing should continue to sell the custom cello.
Question: How should Philby Manufacturing proceed if the price of the custom cello cannot exceed $900?
If the custom cello at a price of $900 sells 100 units per year, then the unit contribution is:

	Unit	Volume per Unit	Total
Revenue	100	$ 900	$ 90,000
Variable cost: Direct material	100	$ 375	$ 37,500
Direct labor	100	$ 240	$ 24,000
Contribution: Revenue — Variable cost	100	$ 285	$ 28,500
Overhead: Fixed cost	100	$ 435	$ 43,500
Gross profit: Contribution — Fixed cost	100	−$ 150	−$ 15,000
If custom cellos are not sold, fixed cost is still paid		−$ 435	−$ 43,500
When custom cellos sell at $900	100	−$ 150	−$ 15,000

Therefore, even at a unit price of $900, it is still better to sell the custom cello than to discontinue it.
Question: At a selling price of $1,000 each, what is the breakeven unit volume for the custom cello?
The breakeven unit volume formula is fixed cost/unit contribution.

The custom cello fixed cost is	$ 43,500
The custom cello unit contribution is unit selling price less variable cost	1,000 − 615
Which is	$ 385
Therefore the breakeven volume in units is	43,500/385, 113 units

Exhibit 13a.5   (Continued)

13a.7 SUMMARY AND CONCLUSIONS

Some items of cost can be traced directly to products, and these items are accordingly called direct costs. Examples are raw materials[2] and factory direct labor. Other items of cost are difficult, or impossible, to trace directly to products. Examples of these items are factory telephone expenses, factory utility costs, or depreciation of factory buildings and equipment. Since these items cannot be directly traced, they are allocated to products by means of one or more other techniques.

These techniques may be simple or complex, accurate or inaccurate, and expensive or inexpensive. Inexpensive, simple techniques include traditional cost assignment like use of direct labor hours as a basis for allocating indirect manufacturing costs. Using traditional allocators like direct labor hours is accurate if manufacturing costs actually are governed by direct labor hours. In this case, traditional allocators like direct labor hours have the virtue of being both accurate and inexpensive. But if manufacturing costs actually are unrelated to direct labor hours, then the traditional allocator will be inaccurate, and is likely to lead to poor decisions relating to product mix, product pricing, and product promotion. The final result may be as catastrophic as organizational failure and bankruptcy.

For this reason, larger organizations are likely to employ more accurate and more expensive methods of cost allocation such as activity-based costing. Activity-based costing requires initial studies to be made regarding the drivers that influence the costs of manufacturing. These studies often tend to be lengthy, detailed, and expensive. In addition to the initial studies required to establish an accurate activity-based costing system, it is advisable from time to time to review the cost drivers in order to verify that they continue to be accurate. Alternatively, outdated cost drivers may become inaccurate over time, and require new studies to find new cost drivers.

---

[2] An exception might be low-cost items such as paper clips, glue, or scraps of cloth that workers use to wipe greasy hands. Generally such items are not worth tracing to products, and are therefore tossed into an indirect category of cost that will be allocated to products, rather than being directly traced to products.

Therefore it is common to find less accurate and also less expensive cost allocation systems in smaller and newer organizations. By the same token, it is common to find more accurate and also more expensive cost allocation systems in larger and older organizations. The latter are more likely to be able to afford more expense and to require superior accuracy. As the old saying goes, "you get what you pay for," or perhaps more to the point, "you get no more than what you pay for."

13a.8 REFERENCES

See the books and video references that follow for further information.

BOOKS

Boyd, Kenneth. *Cost Accounting for Dummies*. Hoboken, NJ: John Wiley & Sons, 2013.

Bragg, Steven M. *Cost Accounting Fundamentals: Essential Concepts and Examples*, 3rd ed. Amazon Digital Services, 2012, www.amazon.com/tag/digital%20downloads/products.

Hansen, Don R., and Maryanne M. Mowen. *Cornerstones of Cost Management*. Independence, KY: Cengage Learning, 2012.

Hansen, Don R., Maryanne M. Mowen, and Liming Guan. Cost Management: Accounting and Control, *6th ed.* Mason, OH: South-Western College Publishing, 2007.

Kinney, Michael R., and Cecily A. Raiborn. Cost Accounting: Foundations and Evolutions, *9th ed.* Mason, OH: Cengage South-Western Publishing Co., 2012.

VIDEOS

Cost Allocation
www.youtube.com/watch?v=fp58HxrTjvY
Aug. 20, 2011—Uploaded by David Alfaro

www.youtube.com/watch?v=vFYAOcwR25M
May 25, 2012—Uploaded by iNinjaNotes

4th Challenge in PM: Cost Allocation
www.youtube.com/watch?v=kfqdn7LL8uA
Mar. 10, 2009—Uploaded by Ion Vaciu

Support Cost Allocation Using Direct Method (Managerial Accounting Series)
www.youtube.com/watch?v=5M8UEZHRN6Y
May 25, 2012—Uploaded by iNinjaNotes

"Cost Accounting 17D Indirect Cost Allocation" Job Cost Sheets, WIP, Support Costs
www.youtube.com/watch?v=tqpfMCvZPwY
Mar. 13, 2013—Uploaded by kenboydstl

Video 1 Cost Allocation
www.youtube.com/watch?v=ZEhSDKM-z1A
Apr. 24, 2012—Uploaded by MoodleMBA

Activity Based Costing—Allocating Overhead (Managerial Accounting Series)
www.youtube.com/watch?v=HINEtWCztVk
Mar. 8, 2012—Uploaded by iNinjaNotes

Activity Based Costing Examples—Managerial Accounting Video
www.youtube.com/watch?v=7SNjEHIYjns
Jun. 13, 2012—Uploaded by Brian Routh TheAccountingDr

Managerial Accounting (Simple Costing, Overhead Cost Allocation)—Divya Anantharaman
www.youtube.com/watch?v=A4xRLbCPBac
Apr. 15, 2013—Uploaded by rutgersweb

What Is Activity Based Costing?—Managerial Accounting Video
www.youtube.com/watch?v=P2wU1d_vhW4
Jun. 12, 2012—Uploaded by Brian Routh TheAccountingDr

Activity Based Costing (ABC) Video #2
www.youtube.com/watch?v=Yrdy8DTS_rM
Mar. 13, 2013—Uploaded by Amanda Russell

CHAPTER 31

REAL ESTATE AND CONSTRUCTION (ADDENDUM)

Benedetto Bongiorno, CPA, CRE
Natural Decision Systems, Inc.

31.11 REPORTING ON A LIQUIDATION BASIS AND DISCONTINUED OPERATIONS

Although decision-making power and economics are now included in the U.S. generally accepted accounting principles (GAAP) definition of control, that definition applies to only certain entities. The Financial Accounting Standards Board (FASB) is working to better align its consolidation models and achieve appropriate consolidation outcomes. However, the changes currently being contemplated would retain the two primary consolidation models.

The standard requires an entity to prepare its financial statements using the liquidation basis of accounting when liquidation is imminent, such as when:

- A plan for liquidation has been approved by the person or persons with the authority to make such a plan effective and the likelihood is remote that the execution of the plan will be blocked by other parties or the entity will return from liquidation, or
- A plan for liquidation is imposed by other forces, and the likelihood is remote that the entity will return from liquidation.

On April 12, 2013, the FASB issued an exposure draft of consequential amendments to the Accounting Standards Codification (ASC) that would result from its financial instruments classification and measurement proposal. The new exposure draft serves as a companion document to the FASB's proposal issued on February 14, 2013.

The amendments in this proposed update would change the requirements for reporting discontinued operations in Subtopic 205-20, which would increase convergence of the requirements for reporting discontinued operations in Subtopic 205-20 and IFRS 5, *Non-current Assets Held for Sale and Discontinued Operations*. A discontinued operation would be either of the following:

- A *component of an entity* or a group of components of an entity that represents a separate major line of business or major geographical area of operations that either has been disposed of or is part of a single coordinated plan to be classified as held for sale in accordance with the criteria in paragraph 360-10-45-9, or

- A business that, on acquisition, meets the criteria in paragraph 360-10-45-9 to be classified as held for sale.

A *component of an entity* comprises operations and cash flows that can be clearly distinguished, operationally and for financial reporting purposes, from the rest of the entity. A component of an entity may be a reportable segment or an operating segment, a reporting unit, a subsidiary, or an asset group.

CHAPTER 33

STATE AND LOCAL GOVERNMENT ACCOUNTING (REVISED)

Cynthia Pon, CPA
Macias Gini O'Connell LLP

Richard A. Green, CPA
Macias Gini O'Connell LLP

Caroline H. Walsh, CPA
Macias Gini O'Connell LLP

33.4 GOVERNMENTAL ACCOUNTING PRINCIPLES AND PRACTICES

(g) TYPES AND NUMBER OF FUNDS.

(iii) Fiduciary Funds. *Replaces text on pages 33 · 22 through 33 · 24 in main edition*

The purpose of fiduciary (trust and agency) funds is to account for assets held by a governmental unit in a trustee capacity or as an agent for other individuals, private organizations, or other governmental units.

Usually in existence for an extended period of time, trust funds deal with substantial vested interests and involve complex administrative problems. The government's records must provide adequate information to permit compliance with the terms of the trust as defined in the trust document, statutes, ordinances, or governing regulations.

Pension (and Other Employee Benefit) Trust Funds. In the pension (and other employee benefit) trust funds, governments account for resources held for the future retirement and other postemployment benefits (defined benefits and defined contribution benefits) of their employees. The resources of these funds are the members' contributions, contributions from the government employer, and earnings on investments in authorized investments. The expenses are the authorized retirement allowances and other benefits, refunds of contributions to members who resign prior to retirement, and administrative expenses. Professional actuaries make periodic actuarial studies of the retirement systems and compute the amounts that should be provided so that the benefits can be paid as required.

The proper accounting for pension trust funds has been on the agenda of the Government Accounting Standards Board (GASB) since its creation. The current GASB guidance in effect on pensions and other postemployment employee benefits (OPEB) includes: Statement No. 25, *Financial Reporting for Defined Benefit Pension Plans and Note Disclosures for Defined Contribution Plans*; Statement No. 27, *Accounting for Pensions by State and Local Government Employers*; Statement No. 43, *Financial Reporting for Postemployment Benefit Plans Other Than Pension Plans*; Statement No. 45, *Accounting and Financial Reporting by Employers for Postemployment Benefits Other Than Pensions*; and Statement No. 50, *Pension Disclosures—an Amendment of GASB Statements No. 25 and No. 27*. Statements No. 25 and 43 address issues related to accounting by pension and other employee benefit plans and pension and other employee benefit trust funds. Statements No. 27 and 45 address accounting and financial reporting for those employers that participate in pension and other employee benefit plans.

Statements No. 25 and 43 describe two basic financial statements for pension (and other employee benefit) plans: the statement of plan net assets and the statement of changes in plan net assets. These two financial statements are designed to provide current information about plan assets and financial activities. Statements No. 25 (as amended by No. 50) and 43 have other requirements for note disclosure that include a brief plan description, a summary of significant accounting principles, and information about contributions, legally required reserves, investment concentrations, funded status of the plan as of the most recent actuarial valuation date, and the actuarial methods and significant assumptions used in the most recent actuarial valuation.

Statements No. 27 and 45 are directed at employers that participate in pension (and other employee benefit) plans and reflect two underlying principles: (1) the pension or OPEB cost recognized should be related to the annual required contribution (ARC) as determined by an actuary for funding purposes; and (2) the actuarial methods and assumptions used by employers should be consistent with those used by the plan in its separate reporting.

In implementing these basic principles, Statements No. 27 and 45 require the ARC to be recognized as pension or OPEB expense in government-wide financial statements and the proprietary funds. Governmental funds will recognize pension expenditure to the extent that the ARC is expected to be liquidated with expendable available resources. If an employer does not contribute the ARC (or has contributed in excess of the ARC), pension or OPEB expense no longer equals the ARC. In these cases, the ARC is adjusted to remove the effects of the actuarial adjustments included in the ARC and to reflect interest on previous under- or overfunding.

Although Statements No. 27 and 45 try to minimize the differences between accounting for pensions (and other employee benefits) and funding pensions (and other employee benefits), they do place certain limits, or parameters, on the actuary's modified calculation of the ARC. These parameters are consistent with those established for accounting for the plan itself in Statements No. 25 and 43. These parameters relate to the pension/OPEB obligation, actuarial assumptions, economic assumptions, actuarial cost method, actuarial valuation of assets, and amortization of unfunded actuarial accrued liability.

Statements No. 27 and 45 establish disclosure requirements that vary depending on whether the government merely participates in a pension (and other employee benefits) plan administered by another entity or includes one or more pension (and other employee benefits) trust funds. Disclosure requirements also vary for governments with a pension (and other employee benefits) trust fund based on whether the pension (and other employee benefits) plan issues separate publicly available financial statements. These disclosure requirements generally include a plan description, funding policy, pension or OPEB cost components, actuarial valuation information, and trend data.

Resources accumulated for OPEB should be accounted for in a separate trust fund from resources accumulated for pension benefits.

Since the effective dates of Statements Nos. 25 and 27, there has been significant debate over the theoretical foundations of pension accounting in the public sector. As a result, GASB decided in 2006 that it would perform a comprehensive review of financial reporting by and for pension and postemployment benefit plans in the United States. The project began in earnest in 2008 with a review of existing standards. In June 2012, GASB issued two statements that fundamentally alter pension accounting and financial reporting rules for state and local governments. GASB Statement

No. 67, *Financial Reporting for Pension Plans, an Amendment of GASB Statement No. 25*, and GASB Statement No. 68, *Accounting and Financial Reporting for Pensions, an Amendment of GASB Statement No. 27*, include significant amendments to the prior pension standards to improve how the costs and obligations associated with the pension benefits that governments provide to their employees are calculated and reported. GASB Statement No. 68 primarily relates to reporting by governments that provide pensions to their employees, and GASB Statement No. 67 addresses the reporting by the pension plans that administer those benefits.

Key changes of these new pension standards include:

- Separating how the accounting and financial reporting is determined from how pensions are funded.

- Employers with defined benefit pension plans administered as trusts or equivalent arrangements will recognize a net pension liability to be measured as the portion of the present value of projected benefit payments to current and inactive employees that is attributed to those employees' past periods of service (total pension liability), less the amount of the pension plan's fiduciary net position.

- Incorporating ad hoc cost-of-living adjustments and other ad hoc postemployment benefit changes into projections of benefit payments, if an employer's past practice and future expectations of granting them indicate they are essentially automatic.

- Immediate recognition of more components of pension expense than is currently required, including the effect on the pension liability of changes in benefit terms, rather than deferral and amortization over as many as 30 years, which is common for funding purposes.

- Use of a single discount rate that reflects (1) the expected long-term rate of return on pension plan investments to projected benefit payments for which the pension plan's fiduciary net position is sufficient to make projected benefit payments, and the pension plan assets are expected to be invested using a strategy to achieve that return, and (2) a yield or index rate for 20-year, tax-exempt general obligation municipal bonds with an average rating of AA/Aa or higher to projected benefit payments to the extent that the conditions in (1) are not met.

- A single actuarial cost allocation method—"entry age normal"—rather than the current choice among six actuarial cost methods.

- Requiring governments participating in cost-sharing multiple employer pension plans to record a liability equal to their proportionate share of any net pension liability for the cost-sharing plan as a whole.

- Requiring governments in all types of covered pension plans to present more extensive note disclosures and required supplementary information.

Federal regulators including the U.S. Securities and Exchange Commission (SEC) have recently increased scrutiny of state and local government pension reporting. For example, in August 2010, the SEC for the first time charged a state, the State of New Jersey, with violating federal securities laws. The SEC alleged that the State of New Jersey was negligent in preparing disclosure documents with respect to its municipal bonds, resulting in material misrepresentations and omissions regarding the funding and financial condition of its two largest defined benefit pension plans. New Jersey agreed to settle the SEC case without admitting or denying the agency's findings. In another example, in October 2010, public officials paid fines that were part of an SEC securities fraud suit settlement against certain City of San Diego officials over their roles in the preparation of pension fund disclosures. The suit alleged that the officials knew the city had significant unfunded pension plan and retiree health care benefits liabilities, and that the city was deliberately underfunding its annual pension plan payments so that it could increase employee benefits while deferring costs. The individuals did not admit or deny the SEC allegations but agreed to pay fines.

Lawmakers are also concerned about public-sector pensions. Legislation introduced in the U.S. House of Representatives in December 2010 and a companion measure introduced by the U.S. Senate in April 2011 would require state and local governments with public-sector pension plans to file annual reports, including funded status information, with the secretary of the U.S.

Treasury Department. Failure to file would bar a government from issuing new tax-exempt, tax-credit, or direct-pay bonds until it filed its report.

Investment Trust Funds.   Investment trust funds should be used by the sponsoring government to report the external part of investment pools, as required by GASB Statement No. 31, paragraph 18.

Private-Purpose Trust Funds.   Private-purpose trust funds, such as one used to report escheat property, should be used to report all other trust arrangements under which principal and income benefit individuals, private organizations, or other governments.

Agency Funds.   Used by governments to handle cash resources held in an agent capacity, agency funds require relatively simple administration. The typical agency funds used by state and local governments include: (1) tax collection funds, under which one local government collects a tax for an overlapping governmental unit and remits the amount collected less administrative charges to the recipient, and (2) payroll withholdings, under which the government collects the deductions and periodically remits them in a lump sum to the appropriate recipient.

APPENDIX: PRONOUNCEMENTS ON STATE AND LOCAL GOVERNMENT ACCOUNTING

Replaces text on pages 33 · 69 through 33 · 75 in main edition

	Government Accounting Standards Board	**Effective Date**
Statement No. 1	Authoritative Status of NCGA Pronouncements and AICPA Industry Audit Guide	On issuance (July 1984)
Statement No. 2	Financial Reporting of Deferred Compensation Plans Adopted under the Provisions of Internal Revenue Code Section 457	Superseded by GASB Statement No. 32
Statement No. 3	Deposits with Financial Institutions, Investments (Including Repurchase Agreements), and Reverse Repurchase Agreements	Financial statements for periods ending after February 15, 1986
Statement No. 4	Applicability of FASB Statement No. 87, "Employers' Accounting for Pensions," to State and Local Governmental Employers	Superseded by GASB Statement No. 27
Statement No. 5	Disclosure of Pension Information by Public Employee Retirement Systems and State and Local Governmental Employers	Financial reports issued for fiscal years beginning after December 15, 1986
Statement No. 6	Accounting and Financial Reporting for Special Assessments	Financial statements for periods beginning after June 15, 1987
Statement No. 7	Advance Refundings Resulting in Defeasance of Debt	Fiscal periods beginning after December 15, 1986
Statement No. 8	Applicability of FASB Statement No. 93, "Recognition of Depreciation by Not-for-Profit Organizations," to Certain State and Local Governmental Entities	Superseded by GASB Statement No. 35
Statement No. 9	Reporting Cash Flows of Proprietary and Nonexpendable Trust Funds and Governmental Entries That Use Proprietary Fund Accounting	Fiscal periods beginning after December 15, 1989
Statement No. 10	Accounting and Financial Reporting for Risk Financing and Related Insurance Issues	Pools—fiscal periods beginning after June 15, 1990 Other—fiscal periods beginning after June 15, 1993

	Government Accounting Standards Board	Effective Date
Statement No. 11	Measurement Focus and Basis of Accounting—Governmental Fund Operating Statements	Superseded by GASB Statement No. 34
Statement No. 12	Disclosure of Information on Postemployment Benefits Other Than Pension Benefits by State and Local Governmental Employers	Superseded by GASB Statement No. 45
Statement No. 13	Accounting for Operating Leases with Scheduled Rent Increases	Leases with terms beginning after June 30, 1990
Statement No. 14	The Financial Reporting Entity	Fiscal periods beginning after December 15, 1992
Statement No. 15	Governmental College and University Accounting and Financial Reporting Models	Superseded by GASB Statement No. 35
Statement No. 16	Accounting for Compensated Absences	Fiscal periods beginning after June 15, 1993
Statement No. 17	Measurement Focus and Basis of Accounting—Governmental Fund Operating Statements: Amendment of Effective Dates of GASB Statement No. 11 and Related Statements	Immediately
Statement No. 18	Accounting for Municipal Solid Waste Landfill Closure and Post-Closure Care Costs	Fiscal periods beginning after June 15, 1993
Statement No. 19	Governmental College and University Omnibus Statement—An Amendment of GASB Statements No. 10 and 15	Superseded by GASB Statement No. 35
Statement No. 20	Accounting and Financial Reporting for Proprietary Funds and Other Governmental Entities That Use Proprietary Fund Accounting	Fiscal periods beginning after December 15, 1993, will be superseded by GASB Statement No. 62, when effective
Statement No. 21	Accounting for Escheat Property	Fiscal periods beginning after June 15, 1994
Statement No. 22	Accounting for Taxpayer-Assessed Tax Revenues in Governmental Funds	Superseded by GASB Statement No. 33
Statement No. 23	Accounting and Financial Reporting for Refundings of Debt Reported by Proprietary Activities	Fiscal periods beginning after June 15, 1994
Statement No. 24	Accounting and Financial Reporting for Certain Grants and Other Financial Assistance	Fiscal periods beginning after June 15, 1995
Statement No. 25	Financial Reporting for Defined Benefit Pension Plans and Note Disclosures for Defined Contribution Plans	Fiscal periods beginning after June 15, 1996; Statement No. 26 must be implemented simultaneously
Statement No. 26	Financial Reporting for Postemployment Healthcare Plans Administered by Defined Benefit Pension Plans	Superseded by GASB Statement No. 43
Statement No. 27	Accounting for Pensions by State and Local Governmental Employers	Fiscal periods beginning after June 15, 1997
Statement No. 28	Accounting and Financial Reporting for Securities Lending Transactions	Fiscal periods beginning after December 15, 1995
Statement No. 29	The Use of Not-for-Profit Accounting and Financial Reporting Principles by Governmental Entities	Fiscal periods beginning after December 15, 1995
Statement No. 30	Risk Financing Omnibus	Fiscal periods beginning after June 15, 1996
Statement No. 31	Accounting and Financial Reporting for Certain Investments and for External Investment Pools	Fiscal periods beginning after June 15, 1997

(Continues)

	Government Accounting Standards Board	Effective Date
Statement No. 32	Accounting and Financial Reporting for Internal Revenue Code Section 457 Deferred Compensation Plans	Earlier of fiscal periods beginning after December 31, 1998, or amendment of the IRC Section 457 Plan
Statement No. 33	Accounting and Financial Reporting for Nonexchange Transactions	Periods beginning after June 15, 2000
Statement No. 34	Basic Financial Statements—and Management's Discussion and Analysis—for State and Local Governments	[1]
Statement No. 35	Basic Financial Statements—and Management's Discussion and Analysis—for Public Colleges and Universities: Amendment of GASB Statement No. 34	[2]
Statement No. 36	Recipient Reporting for Certain Shared Nonexchange Revenues: Amendment of GASB Statement No. 33	Simultaneously with Statement No. 33
Statement No. 37	Basic Financial Statements—and Management's Discussion and Analysis—for State and Local Governments: Omnibus	[3]
Statement No. 38	Certain Financial Statement Note Disclosures Discussion and Analysis—for State and Local Governments	[1]
Statement No. 39	Determining Whether Certain Organizations Are Component Units	Periods beginning after June 15, 2003
Statement No. 40	Deposit and Investment Risk Disclosures—An Amendment of GASB Statement No. 3	Periods beginning after June 15, 2004
Statement No. 41	Budgetary Comparison Schedules—Perspective Differences—An Amendment of GASB Statement No. 34	Simultaneously with Statement 34
Statement No. 42	Accounting and Financial Reporting for Impairment of Capital Assets and for Insurance Recoveries	Periods beginning after December 15, 2004
Statement No. 43	Financial Reporting for Postemployment Benefit Plans Other Than Pension Plans	Effective in three phases based on a government's total annual revenues in the first fiscal year ending after June 15, 1999: for periods beginning after December 15, 2005, 2006, and 2007
Statement No. 44	Economic Condition Reporting—The Statistical Section—An Amendment of NCGA Statement 1	Statistical sections prepared for periods beginning after June 15, 2005
Statement No. 45	Accounting and Financial Reporting by Employers for Postemployment Benefits Other Than Pensions	Effective in three phases based on a government's total annual revenues in the first fiscal year ending after June 15, 1999: for periods beginning after December 15, 2006, 2007, and 2008
Statement No. 46	Net Assets Restricted by Enabling Legislation—An Amendment of GASB Statement No. 34	Periods beginning after June 15, 2005

	Government Accounting Standards Board	Effective Date
Statement No. 47	Accounting for Termination Benefits	For termination benefits provided through an existing defined benefit OPEB plan, the provisions of this Statement should be implemented simultaneously with the requirements of Statement 45; for all other termination benefits, this Statement is effective for financial statements for periods beginning after June 15, 2005
Statement No. 48	Sales and Pledges of Receivables and Future Revenues and Intra-Entity Transfers of Assets and Future Revenues	Periods beginning after December 15, 2006
Statement No. 49	Accounting and Financial Reporting for Pollution Remediation Obligations	Periods beginning after December 15, 2007
Statement No. 50	Pension Disclosures—An Amendment of GASB Statements No. 25 and No. 27	Periods beginning after June 15, 2007, except for requirements related to the use of the entry age actuarial cost method for the purpose of reporting a surrogate funded status and funding progress of plans that use the aggregate actuarial cost method, which are effective for periods for which the financial statements and RSI contain information resulting from actuarial valuations as of June 15, 2007, or later
Statement No. 51	Accounting and Financial Reporting for Intangible Assets	Periods beginning after June 15, 2009
Statement No. 52	Land and Other Real Estate Held as Investments by Endowments	Periods beginning after June 15, 2008
Statement No. 53	Accounting and Financial Reporting for Derivative Instruments	Fiscal periods beginning after June 15, 2009
Statement No. 54	Fund Balance Reporting and Governmental Fund Type Definitions	Fiscal periods beginning after June 15, 2010
Statement No. 55	The Hierarchy of Generally Accepted Accounting Principles for State and Local Governments	Immediately
Statement No. 56	Codification of Accounting and Financial Reporting Guidance Contained in the AICPA Statements on Auditing Standards	Immediately
Statement No. 57	OPEB Measurements by Agent Employers and Agent Multiple-Employer Plans	Provisions related to the use and reporting of the alternative measurement method are effective immediately; provisions related to the frequency and timing of measurements are effective for actuarial valuations first used to report funded status information in OPEB plan financial statements for periods beginning after June 15, 2011

(Continues)

	Government Accounting Standards Board	Effective Date
Statement No. 58	Accounting and Financial Reporting for Chapter 9 Bankruptcies	Fiscal periods beginning after June 15, 2009; retroactive application is required for all prior periods presented during which a government was in bankruptcy
Statement No. 59	Financial Instruments Omnibus	Fiscal periods beginning after June 15, 2010; earlier application is encouraged
Statement No. 60	Accounting and Financial Reporting for Service Concession Arrangements	Fiscal periods beginning after December 15, 2011; provisions are generally required to be applied retroactively for all periods presented
Statement No. 61	The Financial Reporting Entity: Omnibus—An Amendment of GASB Statements No. 14 and No. 34	Fiscal periods beginning after June 15, 2012
Statement No. 62	Codification of Accounting and Financial Reporting Guidance Contained in Pre-November 30, 1989, FASB and AICPA Pronouncements	Fiscal periods beginning after December 15, 2011; provisions are generally required to be applied retroactively for all periods presented
Statement No. 63	Financial Reporting of Deferred Outflows of Resources, Deferred Inflows of Resources, and Net Position	Starting with the fiscal periods that end December 31, 2012
Statement No. 64	Derivative Instruments: Application of Hedge Accounting Termination Provisions—An Amendment of GASB Statement No. 53	Fiscal periods beginning after June 15, 2011
Statement No. 65	Items Previously Reported as Assets and Liabilities	Fiscal periods beginning after December 15, 2012
Statement No. 66	Technical Corrections—2012—An Amendment of GASB Statements No. 10 and No. 62	Fiscal periods beginning after December 15, 2012
Statement No. 67	Financial Reporting for Pension Plans—An Amendment of GASB Statement No. 25	Fiscal periods beginning after June 15, 2013
Statement No. 68	Accounting and Financial Reporting for Pensions—An Amendment of GASB Statement No. 27	Fiscal periods beginning after June 15, 2014
Statement No. 69	Government Combinations and Disposals of Government Operations	Effective for government combinations and disposals of government operations occurring in fiscal reporting periods beginning after December 15, 2013, and should be applied on a prospective basis
Interpretation No. 1	Demand Bonds Issued by State and Local Governmental Entities	Fiscal periods ending after June 15, 1985
Interpretation No. 2	Disclosure of Conduit Debt Obligations	Fiscal periods beginning after December 15, 1995
Interpretation No. 3	Financial Reporting for Reverse Repurchase Agreements	Fiscal periods beginning after December 15, 1995
Interpretation No. 4	Accounting and Financial Reporting for Capitalization Contributions to Public Entity Risk Pools	Fiscal periods beginning after June 15, 1996
Interpretation No. 5	Property Tax Revenue Recognition in Governmental Funds	Fiscal periods beginning after June 15, 2000

	Government Accounting Standards Board	Effective Date
Interpretation No. 6	Recognition and Measurement of Certain Liabilities and Expenditures in Governmental Fund Financial Statements: An Interpretation of NCGA Statements 1, 4, and 5, NCGA Interpretation 8, and GASB Statement Nos. 10, 16, and 18	Simultaneously with Statement No. 34
Technical Bulletin No. 84–1	Purpose and Scope of GASB Technical Bulletins and Procedures for Issuance	None
Technical Bulletin No. 2004–1	Tobacco Settlement Recognition and Financial Reporting Entity Issues	June 15, 2004
Technical Bulletin No. 2004–2	Recognition of Pension and Other Postemployment Benefit Expenditures/Expense and Liabilities by Cost-Sharing Employers	Pension transactions: for financial statements for periods ending after December 15, 2004; OPEB transactions: applied simultaneously with the requirements of Statement No. 45
Technical Bulletin No. 2006–1	Accounting and Financial Reporting by Employers and OPEB Plans for Payments from the Federal Government Pursuant to the Retiree Drug Subsidy Provisions of Medicare Part D	On issuance (June 2006) except for the portions of answers pertaining specifically to measurement, recognition, or required supplementary information requirements of Statement Nos. 43 or 45; those provisions should be applied simultaneously with the implementation of Statement No. 43 or No. 45
Technical Bulletin No. 2008–1	Determining the Annual Required Contribution Adjustment for Postemployment Benefits	Financial statements for periods ending after December 15, 2008
Concepts Statement No. 1	Objectives of Financial Reporting	None
Concepts Statement No. 2	Reporting Service Efforts and Accomplishments	None
Concepts Statement No. 3	Communication Methods in General Purpose External Financial Reports That Contain Basic Financial Statements	None
Concepts Statement No. 4	Elements of Financial Statements	None
Concepts Statement No. 5	Service Efforts and Accomplishments Reporting—An Amendment of GASB Concepts Statement No. 2	None

	National Council on Government Accounting	Effective Date
Statement No. 1	Governmental Accounting and Financial Reporting Principles	Fiscal years ending after June 30, 1980
Statement No. 2	Grant, Entitlement, and Shared Revenue Accounting by State and Local Governments	Fiscal years ending after June 30, 1980
Statement No. 3	Defining the Governmental Reporting Entity	Issued December 1981; superseded by GASB Statement No. 14
Statement No. 4	Accounting and Financial Reporting Principles for Claims and Judgments and Compensated Absences	Fiscal years beginning after December 31, 1982; extended indefinitely by NCGAS 11
Statement No. 5	Accounting and Financial Reporting Principles for Lease Agreements of State and Local Governments	Fiscal years beginning after June 30, 1983

(*Continues*)

	Government Accounting Standards Board	**Effective Date**
Statement No. 6	Pension Accounting and Financial Reporting: Public Employee Retirement Systems and State and Local Government Employers	Superseded by GASB Statement Nos. 25 and 27
Statement No. 7	Financial Reporting for Component Units within the Governmental Reporting Entity	Superseded by GASB Statement No. 14
Interpretation No. 1	GAAFR and the AICPA Audit Guide (Superseded)	Issued April 1986; superseded by NCGAS 1
Interpretation No. 2	Segment Information for Enterprise Funds	Issued 6/80; superseded by GASB Statement No. 34
Interpretation No. 3	Revenue Recognition—Property Taxes	Fiscal years beginning after September 30, 1981
Interpretation No. 4	Accounting and Financial Reporting for Public Employee Retirement Systems and Pension Trust Funds (Superseded)	Fiscal years beginning after June 15, 1982; superseded by NCGAS 6 and repealed by NCGAI 8
Interpretation No. 5	Authoritative Status of Governmental Accounting, Auditing, and Financial Reporting	Issued March 1982; superseded by GASB Statement No. 34
Interpretation No. 6	Notes to the Financial Statements Disclosure	Prospectively for fiscal years beginning after December 31, 1982
Interpretation No. 7	Clarification as to the Application of the Criteria in NCGA Statement, "Defining the Governmental Reporting Entity"	Issued September 1983; superseded by GASB Statement No. 14
Interpretation No. 8	Certain Pension Matters	Fiscal years ending after December 31, 1983
Interpretation No. 9	Certain Fund Classifications and Balance Sheet Accounts	Fiscal years ending after June 30, 1984
Interpretation No. 10	State and Local Government Budgetary Reporting	Fiscal years ending after June 30, 1984
Interpretation No. 11	Claim and Judgment Transactions for Governmental Funds	Issued April 1984; superseded by GASB Statement No. 10

[1] In three phases, based on total annual revenue in the first fiscal year ending after June 15, 1999; Phase 1: governments with total annual revenues of $100 million or more, fiscal periods beginning after June 15, 2001; Phase 2: governments with total annual revenues of $10 million or more but less than $100 million, fiscal periods beginning after June 15, 2002; Phase 3: governments with total annual revenues of less than $10 million, fiscal periods beginning after June 15, 2003.

[2] Public institutions that are components of another reporting entity should implement the Statement no later than the same year as their primary government. For public institutions that are not components of another reporting entity, this Statement is effective in the three phases indicated in the footnote (1).

[3] Simultaneously with Statement No. 34. For governments that implemented Statement No. 34 before Statement No. 37 was issued, Statement No. 37 is effective for periods beginning after June 15, 2000.

CHAPTER 38

ESTATES AND TRUSTS (REVISED)

Philip M. Herr, JD, CPA, PFS
AXA Equitable Life Insurance Company

Elizabeth Lindsay-Ochoa, JD, LLM (Taxation)
Tompkins Financial Advisors

38.1 ESTATES—LEGAL BACKGROUND

Replaces text on pages 38 · 13 through 38 · 19 in main edition

(I) TAXATION OF ESTATES.

(ii) Federal Estate Tax. Decedents with gross estates valued at over $5 million, as adjusted for inflation[1] are required to file a federal estate tax return, Form 706, regardless of the fact that there may be no federal estate tax liability. The federal estate tax is a tax on the value of the decedent's gross estate less certain deductions. Generally, the tax is paid from the estate property and reduces the amount otherwise available to the beneficiaries. Therefore, in the absence of specific directions in a will or trust, taxes are generally apportioned to the property that causes a tax. If property passes without tax because of a marital or charitable deduction, no taxes are chargeable to the property.

The gross estate for tax purposes includes all of the decedent's property as defined in the U.S. Internal Revenue Code (IRC), not merely probate property. Next are listed seven examples of property that is part of the gross estate for estate tax purposes, though not part of the probate estate and thus not accounted for in the representative's accounting:

1. Specifically devised real property
2. Jointly owned property passing to the survivor by operation of law

---

[1] This is the filing threshold effective for decedents dying on or after January 1, 2013, under the American Taxpayer Relief Act of 2012.

3. Life insurance not payable to the estate when the decedent possessed "incidents of ownership," such as the right to borrow or change the beneficiary of the policy, and policies transferred within three years of death

4. Lump-sum distributions from retirement plans paid to someone as a result of surviving the decedent

5. Gift taxes paid by the decedent within three years of death

6. Fair market value of the principal of any revocable living trust of which the decedent was the grantor or settlor

7. Fair market value of the principal of any irrevocable trust in which the decedent, as grantor or settlor, had retained any rights to income, or over the beneficiaries' rights to the use, enjoyment, or possession of the trust principal

In putting a value on the gross estate for estate tax purposes, the representative has an election to value the estate as of the date of death or an alternative date. The alternative date is either six months after the date of death or at disposition of an asset if sooner. If the election to use the alternative date is not made, all property must be valued as of the date of death; if the alternative date is elected, all property must be valued at the alternative valuation date or dates. Alternate valuation is available only if there is a reduction in estate taxes.

Deductions from the gross estate to arrive at the taxable estate include administration expenses (if an election has not been made to deduct them on estate income tax returns), funeral expenses, debts of the decedent, bequests to charitable organizations, and a marital deduction for property passing to a surviving spouse.

The 1976 Tax Reform Act unified estate and gift tax rates by provisions for a unified table to be applied both to taxable gifts made after 1976 and to taxable estates for persons dying after 1976. In computing estate taxes on the taxable estate, gifts made after 1976 are added to the taxable estate and the unified tax is recomputed with credit given for the gift tax previously paid on such gifts. This computation has the effect of treating gift taxes paid as only payments on account of future estate and gift tax brackets. A marital deduction is now available for 100 percent of property passing to the surviving spouse. The property may be left in trust with income to the spouse for life, together with either a general power of appointment or a limited power of appointment. The latter may qualify for the marital deduction if the representative makes a Qualified Terminable Interest Property (QTIP) election with the return. Eventually, the property would be taxable in the surviving spouse's estate, and the tax thereon would be payable from the property.

Estates are also allowed an unlimited charitable deduction for bequests left directly to charities. A prorated charitable deduction is allowed for a split-interest bequest to charity in the form of either a remainder interest or an income interest.

The Tax Reform Act of 1997 added a new exclusion or deduction. Effective for decedents dying after December 31, 1997, decedents who owned a qualified family-owned business interest or family farm may be eligible for this new estate tax exclusion. The amount of the exclusion is correlated with the unified credit, so that in any one year the combination of the taxable estate equivalent of the unified credit and the family-owned business exclusion total $1.3 million. The eligibility rules to qualify for this new exclusion are complex and extensive; therefore, they must be closely reviewed before assuming that an estate will be able to avail itself of this exclusion.

A unified credit is allowed against the computed estate tax. The unified credit is subtracted from the taxpayer's estate or gift tax liability. However, the amount of the credit available at death will be reduced to the extent that any portion of the credit is used to offset gift taxes on lifetime transfers. The amount of the credit is equivalent to a taxable estate of $600,000. Therefore, a decedent can have a taxable estate of up to $600,000 before any estate tax is due.

The Tax Reform Act of 1997 increased the unified credit over a period of years. Beginning in 1998, the taxable estate equivalent to the credit was increased to $625,000, and it then increased as follows through 2006: 1999, $650,000; 2000 and 2001, $675,000; 2002 and 2003, $700,000; 2004, $850,000; 2005, $950,000; and 2006, $1,000,000.

The Economic Growth and Tax Relief Reconciliation Act of 2001 (EGTRRA), signed into law June 7, 2001, made broad, sweeping changes to several areas of the tax law, including the estate, generation-skipping transfer, and gift taxes. In short, the estate and generation-skipping transfer taxes were phased out from 2002 to 2009 and eventually repealed in 2010. That law, however, sunset on December 31, 2010, and taxes became effective again as they were back in 2001. The gift tax was not repealed; however, the rates decreased to 35 percent by 2010. A brief description of the changes made by EGTRRA (while they lasted) is presented next.

The highest tax rate for all three transfer taxes reduced in this way from 2002 through 2009:

2002: 50 percent	2005: 47 percent
2003: 49 percent	2006: 46 percent
2004: 48 percent	2007–2009: 45 percent

In 2010, the gift tax was cut to 35 percent while the other two transfer taxes were zero percent (i.e., repealed). In 2011, the rates returned to the 2001 level of 55 percent when the law sunset. The unified tax credit, or applicable exclusion amount, for the estate tax increased from 2002 through 2009 in this way:

2002–2003: $1 million	2006–2008: $2 million
2004–2005: $1.5 million	2009: $3.5 million

The unified credit, or applicable exclusion amount, returned to the 2001 level of $1 million in 2011.[2] The unified credit, or applicable exclusion amount, was increased to and remained at $1 million as in 2002. This remained constant through 2010, until it returned to the pre-EGTRRA levels.

The qualified family-owned business deduction that was added to the law by the Tax Reform Act of 1997 (discussed earlier) was repealed in its entirety in 2004. It reappeared, however, when the law sunset.

In 2010, Congress passed the Tax Relief, Unemployment Reauthorization, and Job Creation Act of 2010 (TRA 2010). This act allows executors to elect no estate tax for those who died in the 2010 tax year, which allows for the election of the rules under the previous EGTRRA, or to allow the new estate tax law to apply. Therefore, when a person died in 2010, his or her estate or trust had the right to choose if the old law or the new law would apply to the estate. The election to opt out of the estate tax needed to be made on the estate tax return.

This was a unique opportunity for the fiduciaries of estates and trusts of decedents who died in 2010 to elect to follow the law that would be most beneficial to their estate or trust. Generally, the fiduciary needed to decide whether to choose the estate tax and receive the full step-up in basis rather than electing out of the new estate tax law to the carryover basis system. This choice could be important, depending on the size of the estate and other matters, such as whether the decedent owned a life estate in property.

Of course, other considerations would have to be made in deciding which law to apply, as each case must be considered separately. Accordingly, each estate or trust should be closely examined to determine the most advantageous law to apply. Additionally, because Congress acted so late in the year, the federal estate tax return in 2010 was due no earlier than nine months after date of enactment.

TRA 2010 also gives a $5 million unified credit for both 2011 and 2012 with a 35 percent rate. The 2012 rate may be indexed for inflation. If Congress does not pass new legislation, this Act is set to sunset in 2013, with unified credit rates at the 2001 rates.

A significant planning change for clients in TRA 2010 is that individuals who die in 2011 or 2012 would not only have a $5 million exemption available (reduced by any lifetime gifts), but also would

---

[2] The estate tax unified credit exclusion, which was $675,000 in 2001 was scheduled to increase by steps to $1,000,000 in 2006.

have the ability to have any unused portion passed on to the surviving spouse. In fact, a deceased client may not even need to have $5 million in assets to pass $5 million of unused exemption on to a surviving spouse. This is known as the portability of the exemption or unified credit amount.

In 2013, Congress enacted the American Taxpayer Relief Act of 2012. This put to rest uncertainty that has existed in the estate planning world, in the fact that this Act no longer contains a sunset provision. The estate, gift, and generation-skipping transfer tax exemption remains at $5,000,000 and will be indexed for inflation going forward. The unused exemption provision that was set to expire, also known as portability, was also made permanent.

Careful planning is still required. The unused exemption amount is available to the surviving spouse only if an election is made and the amount is calculated on the timely filed estate tax return of the deceased spouse. This means that even if the deceased spouse does not have an estate tax, a federal estate tax return must be filed in order to use the portability provision. This may catch clients with smaller estates who may not necessarily think they need to file an estate tax return. During this time of portability, it may be wise always to file a Form 706 estate tax return to preserve the unused exemption in case the surviving spouse comes into a windfall.

Several other credits may be allowed against the computed estate tax. Most common is a credit for state estate and inheritance taxes (described next). Depending on the nature, situs, and other aspects of certain assets included in the gross estate, these other credits may be allowed against the computed estate tax: prior transfers, foreign death taxes, death taxes on remainders, and recovery of taxes claimed as credits.

Filing of the Form 706 is due nine months after the decedent's date of death. The executor or administrator may request a five-month extension of time to file the return. If any tax is due with the return, an estimated payment of said tax is due nine months from the date of death, with any balance due with the filing of the return.

While payment of the estate tax cannot normally be extended, IRC Section 6166 provides relief for certain estates. Should the estate assets include an interest in a closely held business that exceeds 35 percent of the adjusted gross estate, an election by the executor or administrator would permit the deferral and payment of the estate tax that is attributable to the inclusion of the closely held business interest in the estate in installments over several years. The requirements of this IRC section are strict; therefore, the executor or administrator should carefully consider all available options, advantages, and consequences of making this election.

One of these options, available to closely held corporations, is an IRC Section 303 stock redemption. If funds are available, the corporation may redeem stock held by the executor or administrator equal to an amount that may not exceed the sum of the estate taxes, outstanding debts, and administration expenses. While this option does not serve to defer the payment of estate taxes, it may be used in conjunction with or in lieu of the deferred payments under Section 6166 described earlier.

(iii) State Estate and Inheritance Taxes.   The estate tax in some states, such as New York, takes the form of a tax on the right to transmit wealth that is similar to the federal estate tax. In other states, such as New Jersey, an inheritance tax is applied to one's right to receive a portion of a decedent's estate. The state inheritance taxes are paid from estate funds by the representative, who will therefore withhold an appropriate amount from each legacy or establish a claim against those beneficiaries responsible for the tax by the terms of the will or by state law. Kinship of the beneficiary to the decedent is usually the controlling factor in determining exemptions and tax rates, with close relatives being favored.

Other states, such as Florida, assess an estate tax based on the amount of credit for state death taxes claimed on the federal estate tax return.

Almost all states provide for the tax to be at least equal to the federal credit for state death taxes if total inheritance taxes are less.

EGTRRA reduced the state death tax credit by 25 percent in 2002, 50 percent in 2003, and 75 percent in 2004. In 2005, the credit was repealed and replaced with a deduction for state death taxes actually paid. This required almost every state to enact some form of conforming legislation to coordinate its statute with the federal changes.

The timing of the state's estate or inheritance tax return and payment of any taxes may differ from the federal rules. An executor or administrator should be acquainted with these rules to avoid penalty and interest assessments. A state return may be required to be filed even though no federal return is required and even if no state tax is due.

(iv) Generation-Skipping Transfer Tax. The Tax Reform Act of 1986 revised and imposed a new generation-skipping transfer tax on most transfers made to individuals two generations down from the donor or decedent (i.e., grandchildren). Most transfers prior to 1987 are exempt. Direct transfers or distributions from trusts to individuals two generations down will be subject to the tax if the transfer exceeds the allowable exemption.

A donor/decedent has a lifetime exemption of $1 million. Effective for decedents dying after December 31, 1998, the Taxpayer Relief Act of 1997 provides that the $1 million exemption amount will be indexed for cost-of-living adjustments in $10,000 increments. Transfers in excess of this amount to grandchildren are subject to a flat tax in addition to the estate and gift tax. This flat tax is imposed at the highest marginal estate and gift tax rate, which is currently 55 percent. Consequently, it is conceivable that transferring $100 could cost $110 in estate/gift and generation-skipping taxes. The law is relatively new and complex. Therefore, knowledge of the law and planning are important in order to minimize the impact of the tax.

In 2001, the lifetime exemption was indexed up to $1,060,000. It continued to be indexed for inflation in 2002 and 2003. For 2004 through 2009, the lifetime exemption was equal to the unified credit or applicable exclusion amount. The tax was repealed for 2010 and then returned to the 2001 levels. The tax rate was changed in the same manner as the estate tax rates discussed earlier. In addition, some of the substantive rules were liberalized effective for transfers made after December 31, 2000.

In 2011 and 2012, the exemption was $5 million with a 35 percent flat tax. The exemption is subject to increases for inflation. Going forward, in 2013, the exemption remains $5 million, as indexed for inflation, but the rate is now increased to 40 percent.

(v) Estate Income Taxes. The representative may be responsible for filing annual federal income tax returns for the estate for the period beginning the day after the date of death and ending when the estate assets are fully distributed. The returns are generally prepared on a cash basis and can be prepared on a fiscal-year, rather than a calendar-year, basis. Such an election is made with the filing of the initial return and is often done to cut off taxable income in the first year of the estate. Maintenance of books on a fiscal-year basis and filing the request for an extension of time to file the return will also establish the fiscal year. If returns are not timely filed, the estate will then be required to file on a calendar-year basis.

A federal income tax return is due if the estate earns gross income of $600 or more per year. A $600 exemption is allowed in computing the income subject to federal income taxes. Administration expenses, such as executor's commission and legal and accounting fees, may be deducted if the representative does not elect to take these expenses on the federal estate tax return. If the estate distributes net income (gross income less expenses), such distributable net income is taxed to the recipient, and the estate is allowed a corresponding deduction in computing its taxable income. Any remaining taxable income after deductions for exemption, expenses, and distributions is taxed at a rate specified in a table to be used exclusively for estates and trusts.

The income tax basis of estate assets is stepped up to the estate tax value. Therefore, should the executor or administrator sell any assets to raise cash, the assets' estate tax value is used to determine whether any gain or loss is realized upon the sale. There are, however, certain assets includable in the estate whose income tax basis carries over from the decedent. These assets are called income in respect of a decedent (IRD) and are described in IRC Section 691. Examples of IRD include:

- Proceeds of U.S. savings bonds in excess of decedent's purchase price
- Individual retirement accounts
- Tax-sheltered annuities and regular annuities

- Deferred compensation
- Final paychecks and other remittances of compensation

Certain items of IRD give rise to income taxation upon receipt, while others do not cause taxation until they are redeemed or otherwise liquidated. Should an item of IRD be paid directly to an estate beneficiary or be distributed to the beneficiary from the estate, the same rules regarding income tax basis apply. An offsetting deduction is available to the executor or beneficiary who must recognize IRD in his or her gross income. The deduction is equal to that item's attributable share of the estate tax that its inclusion in the estate has caused.

EGTRRA modified the income tax rules relating to the step-up in basis discussed earlier beginning in 2010. To make up for the loss of revenue from the estate tax repeal, a new carryover basis regime became effective. Under this regime, property acquired from a decedent had a basis equal to the lesser of the decedent's basis or the fair market value of the property on the date of the decedent's death. A total of $4.3 million of property, however, still might have qualified to use the current step-up in basis rules. Up to $3 million of property passing to a surviving spouse, plus up to an aggregate of $1,300,000 of property passing to any beneficiaries qualified for a step-up in basis. These rules sunset after 2010, resulting in the modified carryover basis rules ending and the current step-up in basis rules being reinstated in 2011. Because of carryover basis, better records were needed in order to accurately reflect tax basis in the assets.

Estates must now make quarterly estimated tax payments in the same manner as individuals, except that an estate is exempt from making such payments during its first two taxable years. Accordingly, the penalties for underpayment of income tax are applicable to fiduciaries.

Two pieces of legislation increased the tax rates applicable to estates effective January 1, 2013. The American Taxpayer Relief Act of 2012 increased the top tax bracket to 39.6 percent for taxable income over $11,950. It also increased the 15 percent capital gains rate to 20 percent if the estate is in the 39.6 percent tax bracket. The Health Care and Education Reconciliation Act of 2010 added IRC Section 1411. This section imposes a 3.8 percent Medicare surtax on net investment for estates in the 39.6 percent tax bracket. Investment income includes interest, dividends, rents, royalties, capital gains, and passive income. The net effect of these two tax acts is to effectively impose a 23.8 percent tax on capital gains and a top tax bracket of 43.4 percent on investment income.

Some states also tax the income of estates, and the representative must see to it that such state statutes are complied with.

38.3 TRUSTS AND TRUSTEES—LEGAL BACKGROUND

Replaces text on pages 38 · 31 through 38 · 32 in main edition

(I) TAX STATUS OF TRUST. Unless the trust qualifies as an exempt organization (charitable, educational, etc.), or unless the income of the trust is taxable to the grantor (revocable, or grantor retains substantial dominion and control), the income of the trust is subject to the federal income tax in a manner similar to the case of an individual. In general, the trust is treated as a conduit for tax purposes and is allowed a deduction for its income that is distributed or distributable currently to the beneficiaries. The trust may also be subject to state income taxes, personal property taxes, and so on. A tax service should be consulted for the latest provisions and rulings as to deductions, credits, rates, and filing requirements.

It is important to note that although trusts and estates are taxed similarly, there are two major differences. Trusts must be operated on a calendar-year basis, whereas estates may operate on a fiscal-year basis, usually tied to the decedent's date of death. Second, trusts must pay estimated taxes in the same fashion as individuals. Estates, however, are exempt from this requirement for their first two tax years.

Two pieces of legislation increased the tax rates applicable to trusts effective January 1, 2013. The American Taxpayer Relief Act of 2012 increased the top tax bracket to 39.6 percent for taxable income over $11,950. It also increased the 15 percent capital gains rate to 20 percent if the trust is in the 39.6 percent tax bracket. The Health Care and Education Reconciliation Act of 2010 added IRC Section 1411. This section imposes a 3.8 percent Medicare surtax on net investment for trusts in the 39.6 percent tax bracket. Investment income includes interest, dividends, rents, royalties, capital gains, and passive income. The net effect of these two tax acts is to effectively impose a 23.8 percent tax on capital gains and a top tax bracket of 43.4 percent on investment income.

The impact of the Revenue Reconciliation Act of 1993 (RRA) substantially compressed the income tax rates applicable to trusts and estates. Indexed from its original level effective for tax years beginning in 1993, trusts reached the top 38.6 percent marginal bracket at $9,200 of taxable income in 2002. In 2011, the 35 percent bracket was reached at taxable income over $11,350. Compare this to married individuals filing jointly, for example, where the 35 percent top marginal bracket is not reached until taxable income exceeds $379,150. That is quite a disparity. Trustees of existing trusts need to consider their responsibility to take this disparity into consideration when reviewing the mix of assets in the current trust portfolio and when exercising their discretion to make discretionary distributions of income. In certain cases, where older trusts were established with a different rate structure in mind, and where state law permits, a trustee may want to consider bringing a court proceeding to reform the terms of the trust accordingly. If the settlor is still alive, all of the beneficiaries are adults, and trust is irrevocable, it may be possible under state law, as it is in New York, to revoke the trust and create a new one if the gift tax cost is not excessive.

INDEX